Rock climbing in the Peak District

Rock climbing in the Peak District

Paul Nunn

Constable London

First published in Great Britain 1975
by Constable & Company Ltd
3 The Lanchesters, 162 Fulham Palace Road
London W6 9ER
Copyright © 1975 P.J. Nunn
Photographs by A. Riley. Revisions by P. Burke and P. Nunn
Diagrams and art work by T. Briggs and E. Walker
Second Edition 1977
Third Edition 1983
Fourth Edition 1987
Reprinted 1992
Reprinted 1996
ISBN 0 09 467660 7

Typeset in Baskerville by
Inforum Ltd, Portsmouth
Printed in Great Britain by
BAS Printers Ltd
Over Wallop, Hampshire

Contents

Illustrations

Acknowledgements

Though this volume is an individual effort, it is based both upon long experience of climbing in the area and upon the information which has been supplied to me by large numbers of climbers during the last eight years when, as Convenor of Limestone climbs and Editor of the Official Series of climbing guides after the death of Eric Byne, I had the responsibility for such information. This volume is not intended to replace that series of official guides and indeed could not hope to do so, so great is the co-operative effort required for their production. Thus my debt to the many climbers who have supplied details of their multifarious activities is apparent, as is my debt to my colleagues of the guidebook sub-committee of the BMC Peak Committee.

The format of this book is obviously influenced by Hamish MacInnes' *Scottish Climbs* and it is to him that I owe the recognition that such a volume was possible. Accident procedures are also based upon his expert section on that subject. That this book materialized in an orderly form is primarily the result of my wife Hilary's painstaking efforts.

In different ways, I have been helped by my climbing contemporaries. Alan MacHardy was a hard tutor on gritstone in the late Fifties: Gray West assiduously championed the cause of crumbling limestone and won my sympathy for that much neglected rock; Eric Byne drew me into the onerous tasks of guide work. Finally, my thanks are most particularly due to Tony Riley, who carted his photographic equipment from end to end of the district in concentrated and occasionally frustrating days. Among a host of other individuals, the aid of the following climbers is especially acknowledged for providing either knowledge or, best of all, enthusiasm.

J N R Allen	D Gregory	S Read
W Beech	M Guillard	M Richardson
T Bolger	A Howard	C Rowland
P Braithwaite	E Howard	D Salt
R Brayshaw	C Jackson	D Scott
T Briggs	K Jones	H Smith
A Brooder	T Lewis	I Smith
D Burgess	D Little	J Smith
P Burke	J Loy	J Smith
D Carnell	L Millsom	B Stokes
R Carrington	J Morgan	J Street
R Dearman	D Morrison	B Tweedale
A Evans	J Moss	R Toogood
P Fearneahough	A Moulam	P Watkin
C Foord	D Murphy	B Whittaker
M Frith	K Myhill	K Wilson
L Gillott	A Parker	O Woolcock
D Goodwin	D Peck	A Wright
J Gosling	T Proctor	J Yates

Introduction

No one knows the exact number of recorded climbs in the Peak District. Certainly it exceeds 10,000, a figure which seems large until it is realized that the area is surrounded by some of Britain's most populous urban areas. Climbing, overwhelmingly an activity of urban man, has prospered in these circumstances. As climbers are especially numerous in northern towns, this intense development is hardly surprising. As a result, the Peak District has become, in three generations, Britain's most intensively developed climbing area, with especially heavy development since 1945.

Official guidebooks cover this region's climbs in great detail. Unfortunately it has not been possible to keep this series in print and thus, despite their excellence, the author, as editor of that series, recognized a distinct need for a distillation of what is considered to be the best selection of climbing in the area. It is hoped that such a volume will prove valuable both as an introduction to the area's climbing and as an aid to the regulars, who will probably find such a volume useful with its inclusion of many recent climbs, as yet unpublished, and attractive in its unique photographic coverage. Such a mixture of aims has determined the selection of the 1,100 climbs covered in this book.

A précis of this very complex climbing area demanded a ruthlessness of selection and style of an extreme kind. The results invite criticism and exclude more climbs and even more cliffs than they include. Throughout, there will be routes or cliffs included which would have been excluded by others, but it seems that the reasons for such judgements will differ and that the selection represents a reasonable compromise. An attempt is made to include many of the better climbs in the lower grades, but some will complain of the large numbers of climbs of severe difficulty and above. It is felt that a different selection would not reflect the area's standards nor its usual rock climbing.

The prose style is also savagely curtailed or indeed emasculated to fit the pressures of great quantities of material and little space. History and other details usual in the normal guide are abandoned, and introduction is minimized. It is assumed that climbers can use a map, find the rudiments of survival in these hostile regions and use an ordinary map to travel the area. Those climbers who have longed for less words, more technical guides, should welcome this one, for it is nothing if not that.

The photographs are a response to the need to minimize description, especially of the relationships between the positions of climbs. As far as possible, it is hoped that this will be self-explanatory. Occasionally, in overgrown conditions in the limestone valleys, a little searching may be necessary, but this is inevitable with any guide under such conditions and should not be resented in an adventure sport. The photographs also have an enhancing function – in that respect they form a unique high-quality set with a strong appeal of their own.

No one climber has done every climb in this book. With luck it will shatter the self-deceptions of those who defend inactivity by spurious claims that they have exhausted the potential. For those who have done little, this volume should reveal the immense wealth and variety that awaits their attention. Should someone complete this particular Munro table, his will be a notable effort indeed!

Essentially, despite common views shared by climbers upon the great quality of certain climbs, such a selection from a vast number retains a huge subjective element. Some climbs have been included because they are of fair quality but lie close to those considered to be exceptional. Others which might be slight to the expert are recorded for their value to other climbers. Probably the balance of climbs chosen is wide in geographical scope, while seeming narrow to experts in particular areas because of the author's peculiar and catholic tastes, including, on occasions, a traditionalist enjoyment of walking. The choice remains the responsibility of the author, as do any errors which may have slipped in during the process. Of these and of new climbs or the modification of old ones, he would always like information for inclusion in other editions of this guide.

Paul Nunn   May 1974

The new edition has ceased to cover Walker Barn Quarry which has been virtually destroyed by renewed quarrying. Route description has been substantially revised to exclude unnecessary aid and some of the diagrams have been modified to fit modern practice. A limited selection of new climbs has been included in an appendix. The new climbs are almost all of very high technical standard and reflect the advance which has occurred in the last few years. In the stimulation of that advance, there is little doubt that this volume and particularly its pictorial coverage had a modest but significant part.

Thanks again are due to the numerous climbers who have by their comment helped in the improvement of this volume and to the assiduous editors of *Crags* magazine, which has made the collection of information much easier than was the case in the past.

PJN   March 1977

In the five years since the last edition, the area has increased still further in popularity. Limestone has enjoyed a revival, with standards pushed ahead in the new wave of harder climbs, while grit suffers no flagging of popularity.

Many new climbs have been incorporated into the text and illustrations. Descriptions and grading have been substantially scrutinized and there has been much modification of content with a massive input from Phil Burke. Also a few older climbs, now thought worthy of inclusion, have been brought in. Thus the guide remains an attempt at an overall synthesis with many compromises involved. It is hoped that it remains a useful introduction to the whole area, and that it also functions as an object of discussion and amusement among climbers.

PJN   December 1981

Five years on, the climbing scene continues to change in the Peak and elsewhere. Extremely strenuous, steep technical climbing, especially on limestone, represents the pinnacle of achievement to present leaders of fashion, following trends at Buoux or the Verdon and sometimes using bolt protection. Inclusion of Pic Tor and Rubicon Wall, as well as the modern desperates of Raven Tor, reflect these trends. At the same time, routes like Beau Geste or Gaia are equally vital yardsticks of excellence, and more 'unique' to the Peak in character. In the interplay of grit and limestone lies much of the area's charm, and its capacity to generate new and ever higher levels of climbing achievement. Let us hope that its delights are matched by the imagination and sensitivity of the climbers, and that they continue the best practices from past tradition, as well as welcoming the ideas, strengths, skills and technical methods of future generations.

PJN   December 1986

Notes on the use of the guide

Grades
The usual grading system of the area is used, without internal subdivision, to give the grade for the climb as a whole. Pitch grades are given in the English alphabetical grading system, which is far more readily applied to these climbs than the UIAA system, which crams too many climbs into a narrow band of grades. The extreme grade is subdivided, to reflect a considerable rise in standards which has occurred.

Grading Table

Grade	Abbreviation	English Pitch Grade	UIAA
Moderate	M	1a b c	
Difficult	D	2a b	
Very Difficult	VD	2c 3a	IV
Severe	S	3b c 4a	IV + V −
Very Severe	VS	4a b c	V
Hard/Very Severe	HVS	5a 5b	VI
Extremely Severe	E1–E8	5b 5c	VII – IX
		6a 6b	
		6c 7a	

As always, controversies are likely over the precise grading of pitches and climbs. Artificial climbs are graded on the usual A1– A4 scale.

Abbreviations
P   Piton
PB   piton belay
PA   Piton aid

PR	Piton running belay
FT	Feet
R	Right
L	Left
V	Variation
O/H	Overhand
TR	Traverse

Star rating

Climbs of especially high quality are given a star rating.

* good ** very good *** excellent

General comments

The climbs in this book include many which are technically among the most difficult in the British Isles. The grading in the area is reasonably consistent internally, but visitors should be warned that the peculiar nature of the rock and the extreme pressure of competition in its development has led to ferocious standards of difficulty. Thus some climbs of traditional Very Difficult standard in Derbyshire would merit Severe or even Very Severe in Wales or the Lake District. Many grit or limestone Very Severe Climbs would merit higher grades on cliffs elsewhere; some would merit the highest grades. This is inevitable on local forcing grounds with traditional high standards and a good deal of specialized and peculiar technique developed by their more fanatical habitués. No systematic attempt has been made to downgrade climbs, but the opposite has been done in a few of the more notorious cases of undergrading, especially at the lower standards.

The grading is intended for good weather and refers to climbers wearing PA type footwear, though many climbs can be done in boots. In winter, many of the cliffs become snowbound or very green, sometimes giving very hard climbing.

Where pitons are regarded as necessary they are mentioned. Their use should be restricted and there is a general presumption that they are undesirable on the natural gritstone edges and severely rationed elsewhere. Even less desirable is the chipping of holds, which has recently marred parts of the climbing grounds. Such practices are likely to invite more than disapproval from other climbers.

Proficiency in basic techniques is assumed in attempting different types of climbs. On some routes, especially on limestone, climbers are advised to carry prussik devices, as it is possible to fall into otherwise irrecoverable positions (Sirplum, Chee Dale). If further technical advice is needed, the books in the bibliography may be consulted.

Though details of access are not included, climbers are warned against any practice which is likely to jeopardize the future use of particular crags for climbing. In confrontations, a conciliatory approach always seems to pay whatever one's basic assumptions about property, especially as many farmers have good reason to be antagonized at the depredations of thoughtless 'townies'.

Accident procedure

General
Keep calm. Take time to plan. Prevent further accident. Reassure victim firmly and repeatedly, if necessary. If unconscious, ensure victim is breathing with clear airway, if not *act at once*.

Unconscious patient
Maintain an adequate airway; this is of over-riding importance. If the victim's chest is moving, but he is blue or making choking noises, then the passage of air to lungs may be obstructed by: *teeth, tongue, vomit,* or *blood* running from back of nose, *snow* from avalanche, etc. Open mouth, remove false teeth or teeth knocked out in fall, pull tongue forward and hold chin up and forward. Mop out (or suck out if tube available) any blood, vomit or snow from back of throat and nose with rags, etc. If airway is still obstructed, turn patient gently on to abdomen, head to one side and downhill. Kneel beside patient, facing his head, grasp chest by placing thumbs one on either side of spine, pointing towards his head, fingers round chest. Apply pressure in rhythm with his breathing, and ensure air is passing freely. This also helps to expel any fluids from the airway.

Patient not breathing

Clear airways as above, pinch victim's nose and breathe into
his mouth, making sure chest rises. Do this at normal
respiration rate, until breathing re-starts. If this method is not
evvective, turn onto abdomen and proceed as above.

Stay with patient; keep him warm and secure. *No morphia* or
fluids. After regaining consciousness, the victim can be allowed
to sit up, given a drink and may later walk down, adequately
belayed and supported. Many are unconscious a relatively
short time, but remain confused and irresponsible, thus should
not be left. He may seem back to normal but may later become
confused again or even relapse into unconsciousness. If it is
imperative to leave an unconscious patient, he must be
adequately secured so that he can't sustain further injury or get
lost if he regains consciousness. Mark the place by cairn, etc.,
as there may be no guiding call/signal for rescue parties and in
winter he could be quickly covered with snow.

Dead

The question of death can be very difficult in some cases. If
there is any doubt, artificial respiration and/or external cardiac
massage (by pressing firmly and regularly on the breast bone)
should be carried out, until signs of death are clear or breathing
starts again. Nearly all the commonly used signs of death (e.g.,
no pulse, apparently no breathing, muscular rigidity, pale
'dead-looking' patient) can occur as a result of a drop in body
temperature. Unless the victim has injuries clearly
incompatible with life, it would be wiser to treat him as alive
until expert medical opinion is obtained. The 'apparently dead'
person is in much greater need of urgent assistance than his
injured companion – with say a broken leg. Remember the
gravity of the decision when you decide someone is dead. When
someone dies, blood drains into whatever happens to be the
lowest parts, producing a bluish-red stain in the skin. It will not
be present over areas subject to pressure, e.g., if lying on back,
staining will be present at back of neck, and small of back, but
not over shoulders and buttocks. This staining may be confused
with bruising, but with bruising there is usually localized
swelling and, possibly, skin abrasions.

Morphia

May be given for severe pain and helps in shock and haemorrhage. Never give to someone who has been or is still unconscious – it may kill them. If morphia is given, the patient must be clearly labelled with time and dose.

Wounds

Cover with clean colour-fast cloth, pulling edges together by way in which dressings are applied.

Haemorrhage

Can be stopped by firm continued pressure by a small hand-held pad over the site of wound. Apply pressure for 15 minutes before relaxing. Don't remove pad but bandage firmly in position. Head wounds always bleed freely, but bleeding can be stopped with a light bandage. Pressure should not be applied as this may drive fragments of bone into the brain.

Fractures and sprains

Compare one limb with the other. If in doubt, treat for fracture. Splinting or immobilization prevents further pain, shock and damage, and should be done as soon as possible. Always pad splints: a partially inflated jet splint can be used as padding. If jet splint is used alone, take care to avoid over inflation.

Spine

Symptoms, pain in back and/or cannot feel or move legs or arms. Do not move until skilled help is available (only exception to this is in order to maintain a clear airway). When stretcher arrives, place a soft pad, e.g. pullover, to fill hollow of back on stretcher, if patient is lying on back on ground. If lying face down, put on stretcher in this position. Any movement of spine may result in permanent paralysis.

Limbs

Collar bone and Upper arm: support weight of arm by scarf etc. round wrist and neck. Place hand of injured arm near opposite shoulder and bandage forearm to chest. *Elbow:* do not attempt to bend or straighten arm. Splint as it lies, support weight of forearm. *Forearm and wrist:* improvise splint and strap lower arm to it. Support whole arm in sling, or bandage to body.

Thigh: straighten good leg beside injured leg. If long straight splint is available, place an outer side of injured leg from armpit to below foot and secure to body round chest. Place pads or padded splints between legs and tie both legs and this splint together at knees, ankles and upper thighs. Pass a bandage under injured thigh and up through crutch and tie (to include long splint) to chest bandage underneath armpits. Tie long splint to legs at upper thighs, knees, feet and ankles. *Lower leg or ankle:* slacken boot laces. Proceed as above, but outer splint need only come to mid-thighs. *Ribs:* no emergency treatment necessary.

Frostbite

Superficial: skin white and doughy – heat by applying body heat, e.g., hold affected parts between hands etc. Protect from further cold. Do not rub, or rub with snow. *Deep:* white and hard – do not give any first-aid treatment: keep parts cool.

Exposure

Symptoms: disturbances of speech and/or vision, irrational behaviour, lethargy, shivering, stumbling. Treatment: act at once. Do not allow serious disability or collapse to develop. Prevent further heat and energy loss, e.g., rest, shelter from wind, bivouac sack, windproof clothing to include head and neck. Give glucose, sweet warm drinks, etc. No alcohol. Reassure patient, as fear greatly accelerates exhaustion.

General

Send a competent member of the party for help by a safe route *after* injuries have been assessed, and it is known what type of help is needed. Messenger should leave spare clothing etc. and mark position of patient on map before leaving. He should look back whilst descending to note landmarks. In bad weather, move injured person carefully to a level sheltered place, provided there are no spinal injuries and after other injuries have been dealt with. Place rucksack, ropes, heather or something waterproof underneath, and as many layers as possible on top; massaging uninjured limbs, hands etc. will help to keep circulation going. If victim cannot be moved, keep him warm and sheltered (build snow/rock wall or lie to windward). Slacken boots, but leave on if foot or ankle injured,

otherwise remove. Wrap up feet and place in rucksack to prevent frostbite. Do not give alcohol, but other fluids may be given, provided no internal injuries suspected. In latter case, allow mouthfuls of fluid or chips of ice to moisten mouth and then be spat out. Whilst awaiting stretcher, continue to give distress signals to attract any nearby climbers. *International Alpine Distress Signal:* light, sound etc., six flashes/notes at ten-second intervals, followed by sixty second pause. SOS . . . – – – . . . can also be used. Red flare is also used for distress. *For help dial 999 and ask for police.*

A **National Register of Long Distance Paths** has been set up as a co-operative venture between the Long Distance Walkers' Association, the Ramblers' Association, and *The Great Outdoors* magazine, to help all those involved in setting up walking routes more than twenty miles long in Britain. For further information please write to Miss Sue Coles, Adminstrator NRLDP, 8 Upton Grey Close, Winchester, Hampshire SO22 6NE.

Keith Sharples on Calvary, Stanage (13.2A)

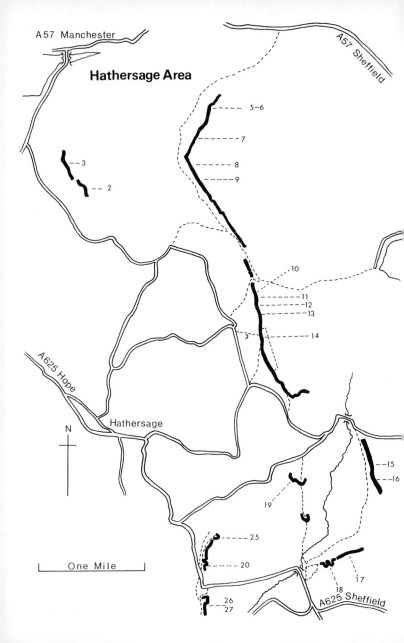

The Eastern Gritstone Edges

The escarpments of the eastern rim of the Peak District form the most continuous series of gritstone edges in England. These edges dominate the upper Derwent valley for almost ten miles, with few interruptions, from Derwent Edge, near Ladybower in the north, to Chatsworth Edge, near Baslow in the south.

They have long been popular with rock climbers, from the early explorations in the late-nineteenth century to the small groups of middle-class gentlemen and unemployed between the wars. (The latter found many of the classic climbs.) Since that time, increasing numbers have only added to their popularity. A pleasant westerly outlook allows them to dry quickly after rain, and in summer the cliffs often become sun-traps. Generally, the rock is not only fairly lichen-free, but more or less completely unvegetated. Most important of all, it is extraordinarily solid on all the natural edges, a delight to expert and beginner alike.

Access

Rail services touch Hathersage and Grindlefore *en route* from Manchester to Sheffield. There are good bus services from the east and south. With private transport, all the cliffs are fairly easily reached in less than one hour.

Camping/accommodation

Campsites:	**High Lees Farm, Hathersage,** for Stanage, Bamford, Derwent, Millstone, Burbage. OS Ref 235835. **Birchens**, OS Ref 276725, for the other more southerly edges.
Bivouacs:	Stanage – Robin Hood's Cave, Plantation Boulders, Froggatt Cave. There are also other less adequate sites on most edges.
Huts:	Bob Downes Memorial hut, Froggatt; owned by the Climbers' Club. There is also a University College of London MC Hut on the Hathersage to Grindleford road, near Leam Hall. The Oread Club have a fine hut at Heathy Lea, near Chatsworth Edge. These huts are not accessible to all comers and must be booked through the respective club hut secretaries.

Derwent Edge – Dovestones Tor   (OS Ref 197898)
Reached in less than one hour from the Bradfield-Strines road,
Cut-throat Bridge or Derwent Terminus, the cliff is gritstone,
quite large, remote and unjustifiably rarely climbed.
Dovestones Tor is the highest central buttress, marked by a
prominent cave at its foot.

1.1   **Central Climb**   75 ft./23 m.   S   (4a)
Start in the cave, TR R just below the roof and reach the ledge
above via groove. Move L to finish up the undercut crack.

*** *1.2*   **The Great Buttress**   65 ft./20 m.   VS   (4c)
Using large pockets, climb L of the cave to a small overhang at
25 ft./8 m. After a move up above this, hand TR R, mantelshelf
and climb the final bulge direct.

** *1.3*   **Brown Windsor**   65 ft./20 m.   S   (4a)
Pull over the bulge by a weathered flake and move up R. Step L
and climb the bulge (birds). TR L until the slab above is
attainable and finish direct.

** *1.4*   **Dovestone Wall**   60 ft./18 m.   D   (2c)
Climb just R of the gully, avoiding difficulty at mid-height by a
slight detour R.

1.5   **Slocum**   35 ft./11 m.   VD   (3a)
Gain the flakes from the L. Climb them and turn the O/H on the
R.

1.6   **Jacobite's Route**   35 ft./11 m.   D   (2c)
A short slab leads to a shallow groove. Escape R above and
finish up the flake on the L.

1.7   **Fennario**   75 ft./23 m.   S   (4a)
Climb a crack R of the cave to a large grass ledge. Up the steep
wall to a small ledge, finishing up the crack above.

---

1   Derwent Edge, Dovestones Tor

1.8 **Gargoyle Buttress**   40 ft./12 m.   VS   (4c)
An easy arête leads to the base of the true buttress. On the R
there is an O/H, which is climbed to a move L on to a slab.
Finish up a steep crack.

Bamford Edge
The prominent gritstone edge, one mile east of Bamford village,
can be reached in less than 30 minutes. It is on private land and
not popular, despite excellent climbing.

Neb Buttress Area   (OS Ref 210846)

2.1 **Virgin Wall – Ontos**   55 ft./17 m.   E2   (6b)
Climb to the bulge and use a flake to reach the wall above. It is
climbed direct.

2.2 **Deep Cleft**   35 ft./11 m.   M   (1c)
The obvious chimney.

*2.3 **Bamford Buttress**   40 ft./12 m.   S   (4a)
Move on to a large flake at 15 ft./4 m. Ascend the wall above on
the L or R.

2.4 **Happy Wanderer**   40 ft./12 m.   HVS   (5a)
Climb the arête direct, with difficulty at the bulge at mid-
height.

2.5 **Auricle**   45 ft./14 m.   E1   (5b)
Climb the wall, left of the thin crack, to the bulge, pull over
direct and TR R below the final prow.

2.6 **Neb Buttress   55 ft./17 m.   HVS   (5a)
Climb the central thin crack (as above) to the bulge, TR L and
climb the edge (wobbly block). With difficulty, pull up the wall
and hand-T R to a strenuous finish. Mid-way between the two
main sections is an isolated undercut arête – Wrinkled Wall, 35
ft./11 m., VS (4c). From the R side of the nose, TR L to the edge
and climb it direct.

2   Bamford Edge, Neb Buttress

Great Tor   OS Ref 208848)

The northern section of the cliff. It is about half a mile from the Neb Buttress Area.

3.1 **Right-Hand Twin**   30 ft./9 m.   HVS   (5a)
Climb R across a perversely unpredictable wrinkled wall to a steep finish.

3.2 Gargoyle Flake   40 ft./12 m.   VS   (4b)
Up the arête to below the flake and layback on good holds to a ledge. Ascend the gargoyle nose direct.

3.3 A35   40 ft./12 m.   E3   (6a)
A ledge under the roof is easily traversed. Use flakes in surmounting the bulge. A weird mantelshelf remains to finish. A lost flake has made this harder.

***3.4 **The Undercut Crack**   35 ft./11 m.   E2   (5b)
The roof is very strenuous, despite good jams. Above it is slightly easier.

3.5 **Hasta La Vista**   30 ft./ m.   VD   (3a)
The flake crack is awkward for its grade. Escape on the R.

3.6 **Recess Crack**   30 ft./9 m.   VD   (3b)
The R corner of the recess is interesting throughout.

***3.7 **Quien Sabe**   45 ft./14 m.   VS   (4c)
Go up the awkward start of Brown's Crack and TR L to the crack on the arête, which requires care.

3.8 **Brown's Crack   40 ft./12 m.   VS   (4b)
There is an awkward start, and interesting jamming above.

3.9 **Curving Crack**   30 ft./9 m.   VS   (4c)
This rather silly-shaped crack saves its crux until the last move!

3.10 **Sandy Crack**   25 ft./8 m.   S   (4a)
The steep corner is taken direct and is awkward to finish.

3   Bamford Edge, Great Tor

Rivelin Edge   (OS Ref 280873)

Situated inside the Sheffield city boundary, the crag is within a few minutes of the A57 road. It has a westerly quarried section and a fine natural edge to the east. The Needle is a unique feature, ensuring it's worth a special visit. The crag is green after rain, though south-facing.

Rivelin Needle

**4.1   Spiral Route   75 ft./23 m.   VS   (4c)

A short wide crack on the south face leads to a ledge. A further thin crack on the R is followed to the platform. From its opposite extremity, follow a horizontal hand-jamming crack, with difficulty, to a small ledge on the w corner (the notch). Attain the summit by a crack which has brittle holds on its extremities.

Descent: By abseil, placed carefully round the summit rock, usually descending to the north side of the pinnacle.

**4.2   Croton Oil   65 ft./20 m.   HVS   (5a)

Take the same start as 4.1 to the ledge. Climb the steep thin cracks to the notch and finish as for 4.1.

**4.3   Blizzard Ridge   55 ft./17 m.   HVS   (5a)

Climb a short wall below the ridge, then R of the ridge before moving on to the edge. Follow this to the top, via an undercut bulge.

**4.4   The Brush Off   35 ft./11 m.   E3   (5b)

Follows the L edge of the buttress, 30 yds./27 m. E of the Needle.

**4.5   Fringe Benefit   40 ft./12 m.   HVS   (4c)

Start as 4.4, but climb diagonally R by a series of sloping holds.

Stanage Edge (OS Ref 226866–247832)

Stanage Edge is four miles long and the most important of the eastern gritstone edges, with a total of over 500 climbs. It is readily reached by walking routes from the A57 at Moscar Lodge; from Bamford and Hathersage in the valley to the west; and by a variety of routes across theHallam Moors from Sheffield to the east. It is possible to drive to within 20 minutes' walk of any part of the crag. The rock is eminently sound.

Stanage End (OS Ref 226866)

*5.1 **The Pinion** 45 ft./14 m. VD (3b)
Climb the L edge of the slab and move R past a hole to a ledge. Follow a short crack and TR R by a larger ledge to the top.

*5.2 **Green Streak** 35 ft./11 m. VS (4b)
The slab is taken direct.

*5.3 **Incursion** 45 ft./14 m. HVS (5a)
Move R from the ledge, a few feet up the slab, and climb the slab on small pockets.

5.4 **Prospero's Climb 40 ft./12 m. VD (3b)
Take the slab centre to a ledge at 20 ft./6 m. Move L and finish by a flake.

*5.5 **Crab Crawl** 40 ft./12 m. S (4a)
Ascend the R edge of the slab. There are several awkward reaches.

6.1 **Doctor's Chimney** 60 ft./18 m. VD (3b)
Up the L side of the pinnacle to the chimney, which yields to classic back and foot facing L.

*6.2 **Surgeon's Saunter** 60 ft./18 m. HVS (5b)
Make very difficult layaway moves to reach the upper cracks, which give a less difficult finish.

4   Neil Foster on Plague, Rivelin

6.3 **The Wobbler**   30 ft./9 m.   HVS   (5b)
Climb the ʟ of the wall, using very thin cracks.

6.4 **February Crack**   30 ft./9 m.   VS   (4b)
Layback and jam the steep corner crack.

6.5 **Old Salt   35 ft./11 m.   HVS   (5a)
Ascend the arête to a ledge and move ʟ with difficulty up the final wall.

*6.6 **Valediction**   30 ft./9 m.   VS   (4c)
A steep impressive crack, finishing direct over the final o/ʜ.

Stanage Marble Wall (OS Ref 225864)

7.1 **Marble Tower Flake**   40 ft./12 m.   VD   (3a)
From the pile of boulders, attain the arête, move ʟ to a ledge and finish by a flake.

7.2 **Terraza Crack**   35 ft./11 m.   HVS   (5a)
Climb the steep narrow crack, passing the bulge with difficulty.

7.3 **Nectar   45 ft./14 m.   E4   (6b, 6a)
Climb the corner direct with great difficulty. Take the roof above to finish.

*7.4 **Orang Outang**   30 ft./9 m.   E1   (5c)
Climb the groove and swing round the o/ʜ to reach the final widening of the crack.

7.5 **Goosey Goosey Gander   40 ft./12 m.   E4   (6a)
Start 20 ft./6 m. ʀ of 7.4. Move ʟ to crack and climb a wall to an o/ʜ crack. Finish up this.

7.6 **Left-hand Tower**   40 ft./12 m.   S   (4a)
Up a thin crack ʟ of the chimney to reach a block. Tʀ a ledge on the ʀ to the easy chimney and finish up its wall. The upper arête is 4c.

5   Stanage End, Green Streak Slab

** 7.7 **Right-hand Tower**   45 ft./14 m.   HVS   (5a)
Take a short crack, then follow the arête to a very rounded
finish.

7.8 **First Sister**   35 ft./11 m.   VS   (4c)
Climb the first crack in the gully wall, just ʀ of the arête, to a
ledge and finish either direct or on the ʀ.

7.9 **Second Sister**   35 ft./11 m.   VS   (4c)
Climb the second crack.

7.10 **Richard's Sister**   30 ft./9 m.   S   (4a)
The third crack is climbed direct.

Stanage – Blurter Buttress   (OS Ref 224854)

8.1 **Overhang Chimney**   55 ft./17 m.   VD   (3a)
Follow the chimney, with difficulty, near the central
chockstones.

*** 8.2 **The Blurter**   75 ft./23 m.   HVS   (5a)
Up overhanging chimney to the o/ʜ, ᴛʀ ʟ to the groove and up
it with difficulty. Move ʀ, up a little, then back ʟ and up the
steep face round the arête.

8.3 **Aries**   30 ft./9 m.   S   (4a)
Climb the groove, taking the crack in the o/ʜ above.

8.4 **Typhoon**   40 ft./12 m.   S   (4a)
From a point a few feet up 8.3, move ʟ and take an awkward
curving crack to a ledge. Finish up rounded rock.

Stanage – High Neb   (OS Ref 229853)

9.1 **Straight Crack**   45 ft./14 m.   S   (4a)
Follow the crack, which grows progressively more difficult.

6/7   Stanage End and Marble Wall (above)

*9.2 Twisting Crack   45 ft./14 m.   VD   (3b)
Climb the crack just L of the O/H, which is awkward in places.

**9.3 Kelly's Overhang   50 ft./15 m.   HVS   (5b)
Leave 9.2 and swing on to a block in the O/H. Stand on this to
reach holds directly above and move R or make a difficult move
R at a low level to better holds.

**9.4 Inaccessible Crack   60 ft./18 m.   VS   (4b)
Pull out of the cave and climb the crack to a ledge, move L and
finish up the steep crack.

*9.5 Impossible Slab   50 ft./15 m.   E2   (5c)
Follow the above route to the ledge. Take the very difficult slab
above by mantelshelf moves.

*9.6 Eckhard's Chimney   40 ft./12 m.   VD   (3b)
The chimney is awkward for the first 20 ft./6 m., with moves on
the L face where it narrows. Above it is easier.

***9.7 Quietus   45 ft./14 m.   E2   (5c)
A steep groove leads to the overhang. Pull on to the slab and
ascend to the O/H. Hand-TR a thin flake to the edge, pull up and
finish using thin parallel cracks.

**9.8 Norse Corner Climb   45 ft./14 m.   S   (4a)
A short slab is climbed to an O/H where a move R is possible on
to better holds and a large platform. A crack follows. It is also
possible to reach the ledge from the R (D, 2c).

9.9 Tango Crack   40 ft./12 m.   D   (2c)
The R hand crack is climbed direct.

***9.10 High Neb Buttress   60 ft./18 m.   VS   (4c)
The buttress R of an easy descent. Start R of the centre of the
buttress. Climb the face for about 15 ft./4 m., move L and up its
centre. The section above is delicate, whether taken on the L or
R. Above it eases.

8   opposite above: *Stanage, Crowchin*   *9*   below: *Stanage, High Neb*

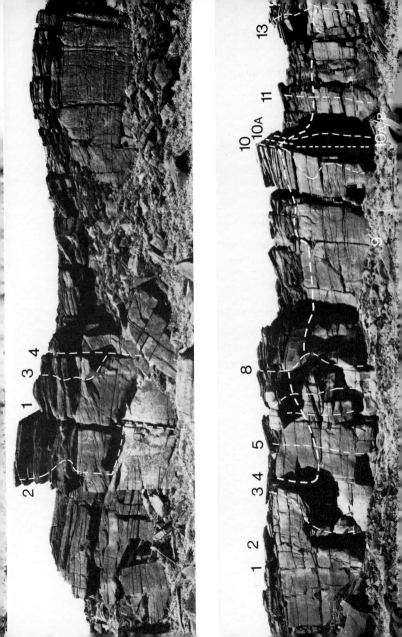

*9.*10A **The Crypt Trip**   60 ft./18 m.   E5   (6b)
A hard start leads to a break and harder moves up the wall above.

***9.10B **Old Friends**   60 ft./18 m.   E3   (5c)
From a point just L of the east corner, go up L via thin flakes to a groove, ascend it and reach the traversing crack. Move R and finish up the wall.

*9.*11 **Mantelshelf Climb**   45 ft./14 m.   D   (2c)
Up the face by a line of obvious shelves.

*9.*12 **Cave Buttress**   50 ft./15 m.   VD   (3b)
Up the buttress front to the O/H, move R and climb awkwardly up the face.

9.13 **Jeepers Creepers   45 ft./14 m.   HVS   (5b)
This route takes the O/H of 9.12 direct by a gymnastic move.

*9.*14 **High Neb Traverse**   320 ft./97 m.   VS   (4b)
This route follows a line at mid-height, including a spectacular hand-TR across the steep face of Neb Buttress.

Stanage – Wall End   (OS Ref 240843)

*10.1 **Fern Crack**   55 ft./17 m.   VS   (4c)
Layback a short crack to the ledge. Pull over the steep section, using side-holds hidden in the crack, and step L to finish.

*10.*2 **Fern Groove**   55 ft./17 m.   E1   (5b)
From the ledge's R end, reach a horizontal crack and TR L to the groove. Enter and climb it with difficulty.

10.3 **Wall End Slab   50 ft./15 m.   S   (4a)
Reach a small ledge from the R. Climb the ledge to a large slanting shelf. TR R and reach the top of the slab by a mantelshelf. Finish up the wall behind.

9.7   Quietus Stanage. Danny Murphy

* V Wall End Slab Direct   40 ft./12 m.   E2   (5b)
From the ledge at 10 ft./3 m., step up R . Pull over the bulge to reach the TR and continue as for the ordinary route. Poor protection.

** 10.4 Wall End Crack   55 ft./17 m.   S   (3a)
Start on the L and climb up to reach the crack on the R. Climb the chimney-crack with difficulty at mid-height.

* 10.5 Wall End Flake Crack   60 ft./18 m.   VS   (4b)
Up the jamming crack and cross a shelf to the R to the base of the twin cracks. Climb them separately or in tandem.

10.6 Helfenstein's Struggle   50 ft./15 m.   D   (2c)
A minor barrier leads to the gully. Climb the L wall and back and foot the cave section.

** 10.6A Saul's Arête – Archangel   65 ft./20 m.   E3   (5c)
Climb the sharp arête by laying-away techniques.

*** 10.7 Goliath's Groove   60 ft./18 m.   VS   (4c)
Ascend direct by jamming and layaway on the final bulge.

V Doncaster's Route   65 ft./20 m.   VS   (4c)
From the midway ledge, move R to a platform. The short wall on the R provides a steep finale.

10.7A Ulysses   60 ft./18 m.   E6   (6b)
Climb the R arête of 10.7 with increasing difficulty. No protection.

10.8 Holly Bush Gully L   60 ft./18 m.   VD   (3b)
A strenuous corner climb on large blocks.

10.9 Holly Bush Gully R   60 ft./18 m.   D   (2c)
Entry is difficult, but the section above eases.

9.10B   *Old Friends, Stanage. Bob Bradley*

** *10.*10   **Fairy Steps**   40 ft./12 m.   VS   (4a)
Use small holds to reach a TR line. Tr L with care to a
mantelshelf and final wall. Unprotected.

Stanage – Tower Face Area   (OS Ref 241842)

*11.*1   **Fina**   45 ft./14 m.   HVS   (5b)
Take a crack to horizontal cracks, TR R and continue direct.

*11.*2   **Tower Gully**   40 ft./12 m.   S   (4a)
The R branch has a bulging finish.

** *11.*3   **Tower Crack**   65 ft./20 m.   HVS   (5a)
The niche is reached by a short crack. The niche crack is
awkward at the exit, and a stance is possible above. Move up a
corner before escaping R by the O/H to a good ledge.

** *11.*4   **Tower Chimney**   60 ft./18 m.   HVS   (5a)
After an easy entry, the funnel-shaped section is knee-wearing
and insecure. Exit R.

** *11.*5   **Tower Face**   70 ft./21 m.   HVS   (5a)
Move up to a weakness and TR R to a friable flake. Move up
near the R edge to a TR line L. (Entry is possible from the R
here.) Step L and layback the flake.

V Tower Chimney and Face   85 ft./26 m.   VS   (4c)
Start up the chimney, but exit R to a delicate TR leading to the
11.5 climb (unprotected).

V BP Super   60 ft./18 m.   E3   (5c)
Climb the face L of 11.5 to a break, move L and up the arête,
then back R to join 11.5.

10   opposite above: *Stanage Wall End*
11   opposite below: *Stanage Tower Face*

Stanage – Paradise Wall Area   (OS Ref 242841)

50 yds./46 m. L is Pegasus Wall.

** 12.1   Pegasus Wall   40 ft./12 m.   VS   (4c)

Up shiny holds to a ledge and climb the wall above quite steeply.

* 12.2   Overhanging Wall   35 ft./11 m.   HVS   (5a)

The edge of the scoop is reached (runner in overlap), Tr r (crux) to the edge and pull up the steep wall above.

** 12.3   Paradise Wall   50 ft./15 m.   VS   (4c)

Climb cracks to a ledge at 20 ft./6 m. Move r awkwardly and climb twin cracks merging before the top.

12.3A   Comus   40 ft./12 m.   E4   (6a)

Climb a wall on tiny pockets.

12.4   Curved Crack   35 ft./11 m.   VD   (3b)

A nose-grinder with little protection.

** 12.5   Billiard Buttress   65 ft./20 m.   HVS   (5a)

Move r up a steep scoop to the horizontal crack. Tr l and delicately ascend the edge until it eases. Poor protection.

12.6   Milsom's Minion   65 ft./20 m.   E1   (5b)

Climb from a block to the horizontal. Move r and climb a bulging wall, using a pocket with difficulty.

Stanage – Unconquerable Cracks Area
(OS Ref 242839)

** 13.1   Namenlos   45 ft./14 m.   HVS   (5a)

A crack leads to a block belay. Move l and ascend the scoop with difficulty.

13.2   August Arête   40 ft./12 m.   HVS   (5a)

Up a crack to the ledge. move r on to the arête, continuing with difficulty.

12   Stanage Paradise Wall

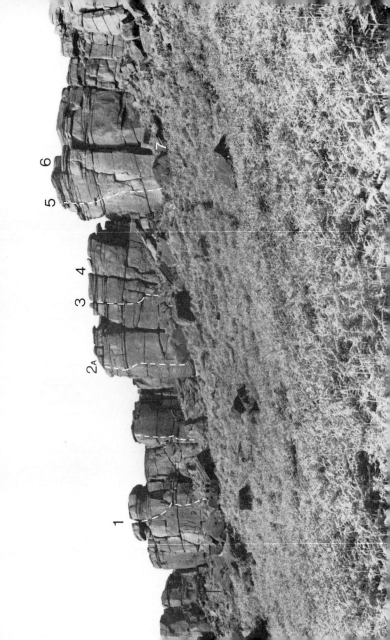

** *13.2A* **Calvary**   50 ft./15 m.   E4   (6a)
Takes the smooth buttress between 13.2 and 13.3. Climb the
crack and move L. Ascend with difficulty and finish up an arête
or direct up the wall.

13.3 **Cleft Wall I**   40 ft./12 m.   VD   (3a)
Climb parallel cracks to a TR L. Finish up the crack above.

13.4 **Cleft Wall II**   40 ft./12 m.   S   (3c)
Take the crack direct.

*** *13.5* **The Left Unconquerable**   40 ft./12 m.   E1   (5b)
Jam to the overlap at 30 ft./9 m.; overcome it (crux) by layaway
and finish more easily.

*** *13.6* **The Right Unconquerable**   40 ft./12 m.   HVS   (5a)
Move out R to the flake and layback boldly to the top overlap.
Move slightly R and use a hidden small hold to pull over.

13.7 **Curving Chimney**   40 ft./12 m.   D   (2c)
Climb direct.

Stanage – Robin Hood and Black Hawk Areas
(OS Ref 243836–247832)

*** *14.1* **Martello Buttress**   50 ft./15 m.   S   (4a)
Pull on to ledge on R and ascend very rounded rock up the
centre, then out L to a ledge. Finish up the arête.

14.2 **Saliva**   40 ft./12 m.   HVS   (5a)
The smooth steep wall is taken diagonally on small holds to the
L arête, up which the climb finishes.

14.3 **Devil's Chimney**   40 ft./12 m.   D   (2b)
Up the back initially, before moving out to exit.

* *14.4* **Hell Crack**   40 ft./12 m.   VS   (4b)
Jam the O/H, and use horizontal jams to overcome rounded rock
above.

13   *Stanage, Unconquerable Cracks*

** 14.5 **Heaven Crack**   35 ft./11 m.   VD   (3b)
Layaway climbing, culminating in a delicate final move.

** 14.6 **Mississippi Chimney**   55 ft./17 m.   VD   (3a)
The first few feet are the most difficult.

*** 14.6A **Dark Continent**   70 ft./21 m.   E1   (5c)
Start just L of 14.7. Climb the wall and pass an O/H to reach the
TR of 14.7. Go straight up the wall and over an overlap to finish
direct over a capstone.

*** 14.7 **Congo Corner**   70 ft./21 m.   HVS   (5b)
Up the thin bulging crack and exit L from the niche, moving
back R and attaining an overhung shelf with difficulty. Make
steep dificult moves to finish. It is also possible to climb the
lower nose direct.

*** 14.8 **Mississippi Buttress Direct**   65 ft./20 m.   VS   (4c)
Up wobbly blocks to the bulge. Move R, and over awkward
bulges to a niche. Positive jams and layaway moves complete
the climb.

V   65 ft./20 m.   HVS   (5a)
Start R of 14.8. Climb bulge and move L to below diagonal
break. Move R and follow rounded cracks to a steep step R to
finish.

* 14.9 **Morrison's Redoubt**   50 ft./15 m.   HVS   (5b)
A ledge is left by a steep move and mantelshelf. Move slightly R
and use a crack to pass a final bulge.

** 14.10 **Balcony Buttress**   55 ft./17 m.   VD   (3b)
An awkward wall leads to a series of rounded cracks R of the
arête, which are followed to a ledge. Pull over a bulge, TR L and
make a steep layaway move to finish.

14.11 **Agony Crack**   35 ft./11 m.   VS   (5a)
Reach a cramped ledge and layaway to overcome the O/H.

** 14.12 **Crack and Cave**   60 ft./18 m.   VD   (3b)
A crack leads to the cave. TR R and finish up the buttress.

*14.13 **Twin Chimneys Buttress**   55 ft./17 m.   VS   (4c)
The buttress arête has a long reach at 25 ft./8 m.

14.14 **Little John's Step**   60 ft./18 m.   VD   (3b)
Climb the detached buttress by the arête and step on to a steep face. From a niche climb a wall to the top of a chimney.

14.14A **Wuthering   60 ft./18 m.   E1   (5b)
Take 14.15 for 15 ft./4 m. and attain a foothold on the L arête. TR L above the roof and climb the wall.

14.15 **Chockstone Chimney   55 ft./17 m.   VD   (3b)
The polished V is climbed by back and foot to the O/H; above, move R and pass a chockstone.

14.16 **Paucity**   50 ft./15 m.   HVS   (5b)
Move L below the O/H and climb a deceptively difficult shallow groove.

***14.17 **Robin Hood's Crack**   60 ft./18 m.   VD   (3b)
Scratched holds are followed past a move R to the cave. Continue up the polished wall on the L.

14.18 **Cave Gully**   35 ft./11 m.   D   (2b)
The upper slot is the more difficult.

***14.19 **Cave Innominate**   55 ft./17 m./   VS   (4c)
The indefinite line of holds on the R edge of the gully gives sustained climbing to a balcony cave. Pull out over the O/H on the L.

14.19A **Last Bolt**   45 ft./14 m.   E3   (5c)
Start R of 14.9. Make a diagonal L ascent to the arête, finishing by arête just R of 14.9.

V Cave Gully Wall   HVS   (5a)
Climb the wall of the twin caves, the upper section being steep and difficult.

* 14.19B Cave Eliminate   50 ft./15 m.   E2   (5c)
Start just R of 14.19A. Move up to a ledge and climb up R to
below bulge. Pull over and finish up the wall. Direct start: 6a.

** 14.20 Cave Arête   40 ft./12 m.   HVS   (5a)
Good holds lead to a steep, difficult move at half-height and
delicate climbing thereafter.

** 14.21 Balcony Cave Direct   40 ft./12 m.   VD   (3b)
The V-groove leads to a bulge which is difficult to pass. The
o/H finish is severe (4a).

* 14.22 Desperation   40 ft./12 m.   E1   (5c)
Make a steep pull up to reach better holds. Move L and climb
the wall direct to an overlap.

** 14.23 Ellis's Eliminate   70 ft./21 m.   VS   (4c)
Ascend the horizontal crack and hand-TR (jams) to the nose.
Finish more easily in an exposed position.

* 14.23A Ginny Come Lately   70 ft./21 m.   E1   (5b)
From the mid-point of the TR of 14.23, climb the wall and slab
direct.

*** 14.24 Inverted V   70 ft./21 m.   VS   (4b)
The first polished crack leads to a bulge (jamming). Climb to a
stance below the roof. Exit R or L.

*** 14.25 Right-hand Buttress   75 ft./23 m.   S   (3c)
A short ascent leads to the TR R and mantelshelf on to a ledge.
The rounded crack above is awkward and sustained.

14.26 Straight Crack   65 ft./20 m.   VS   (4b)
Climb the L-hand side of the chimney and a bulging crack to
easier ground.

** 14.27 Bishop's Route   70 ft./21 m.   S   (4a)
Reach the flake ledge from the R. Climb the upper wall
delicately by one of several exits.

14.14A   Wuthering. Paul Nunn

* *14.28* **The Great Flake**   60 ft./18 m.   S   (4a)
The flake is particularly awkward at the o/ʜ. There is a short wall to finish.

14.29 **Pedestal Chimney**   50 ft./15 m.   D   (2c)
The ʟ-hand crack leads to the ʀ-hand chimney proper. Above it eases.

*** *14.30* **Black Slab**   40 ft./12 m.   S   (4a)
A few steps ʟ lead to a ledge. Climb ʀ to discover the easiest route up the slab centre to a ᴛʀ line at two-thirds height. Go ʟ to the arête and finish direct or by a deviation ʀ again.

V Whillan's Pendulum and Black Magic   HVS   (5b)
An ape-like swing ʀ to reach the first ledge. Climb the arête direct, with long reaches.

* *14.31* **The Flange**   55 ft./17 m.   HVS   (5a)
An initial steep bulge leads to a niche, above which the moves are delicate and poorly protected to a step ʟ near the top.

** *14.32* **April Crack**   55 ft./17 m.   S   (4b)
Avoid the first wide crack on the ʀ, then climb direct by jamming and/or layaway, not omitting some holds on the ʀ near the top bulge.

* *14.33* **Easter Rib**   55 ft./17 m.   E1   (5b)
There is a delicate and unprotected move at 35 ft./11 m.

** *14.34* **Christmas Crack**   55 ft./17 m.   S   (4b)
A sentry box ends in a steep positive crack. The section above can be followed direct or partially omitted by a steep swing ʟ.

** *14.35* **Central Trinity**   55 ft./17 m.   VS   (4c)
The crack ends at 20 ft./6 m. Tʀ ʟ and continue passing a triangular niche (crux).

14.36 **Right-hand Trinity**   50 ft./15 m.   S   (4b)
Climb the crack direct, the small o/H being the crux at 25 ft./8 m. It can be avoided on the R.

14.37 **Green Crack**   45 ft./14 m.   VS   (4b)
The steep corner crack yields to jamming and layaways before a final chimney.

14.38 **Rusty Wall Climbs**   40 ft./12 m.   HVS   (5c)
The lower walls to the R provide at least four difficult extended boulder problems, demarcated to the south by the severe oblique crack (4a).

14.39 **Narrow Buttress**   50 ft./15 m.   VS   (4c)
A crack on the R fades. TR L and climb the buttress, moving R as soon as possible and taking the o/H; on the R.

*** 14.40 **Holly Bush Crack**   50 ft./15 m.   VD   (3a)
Steep moves on blocky rock are followed by a fine layaway crack.

* 14.41 **Queersville**   55 ft./17 m.   HVS   (5a)
Climb a flake until a move L to the centre of the wall. Up to a small ledge and TR R to below a small o/H. Pull over the o/H on to the arête and mantelshelf to a ledge before easier ground.

* 14.41A **Yosemite Wall**   60 ft./18 m.   HVS   (5b)
Climb straight up over an overlap to a ledge. Go up the wall R and over an o/H to finish.

14.42 **Leaning Buttress Gully**   55 ft./17 m.   VS   (4c)
Both angles yield to jam and layback technique.

** 14.43 **Leaning Buttress**   60 ft./18 m.   S   (3c)
The buttress can be reached by a TR from the R at 20 ft./6 m. It is climbed on the L. The first section is HVS if taken direct.

14.44 **Leaning Buttress Crack**   55 ft./17 m.   VD   (3b)
The crack R of the buttress is increasingly difficult and polished.

14.45 **Garden Wall**   45 ft./14 m.   VD   (3b)
A crack or wall to its R leads to the platform. The chockstone-chimney is climbed direct at first, but the stone is avoided on the L, being slightly more difficult if taken direct.

*** 14.46 **Flying Buttress**   65 ft./20 m.   VD   (3b)
The lower slab is climbed by the polished question-mark – up a few feet then R before a step up to the O/H, followed by a TR L to a small ledge. The hanging groove leads to an overhung shelf and pull-over on to the buttress top. A short wall above completes the route.

14.47 **Flying Buttress Overhang**   50 ft./15 m.   HVS   (5b)
Climb the slab to the O/H centre. Climb the O/H direct, the first moves being the crux.

** 14.48 **Kirkus' Corner**   45 ft./14 m.   HVS   (5b)
Swing over the R corner of the O/H to a cramped shelf and continue delicately up the scoop.

14.49 **Grey Wall**   45 ft./14 m.   VD   (3b)
Polished shelves are followed out R and back L to finish direct.

* **V Townsend's Variant**   35 ft./11 m.   VS   (4c)
Follow the R edge of 14.49 and finish magnificently up the edge (unprotected).

* 14.50 **Unprintable**   55 ft./17 m.   HVS   (5b)
A thin crack leads to a crouching cave. Jams are used to get into a layback, which is best done quickly.

** 14.51 **Dangler**   55 ft./17 m.   E2   (5c)
From the cave move R and swing round the long O/H to easier ground.

** 14.52 **Tippler**   65 ft./20 m.   E1   (5b)
The R edge of the buttress is climbed to a TR line at 20 ft./6 m. Go L to the thin crack in the O/H above. Pull over and make an awkward move up the face to the ledges. The direct over the lower bulge is harder (E2, 6a).

14.53 **Y Crack**   55 ft./17 m.   S   (4a)
A strenuous wide fissure in a deep corner.

** *14.54* **Z Crack**   60 ft./18 m.   VS   (4c)
The first crack is overhanging and jammed. A steep little crack
on the L completes the route.

* *14.54A* **Chameleon**   50 ft./15 m.   E3   (6a)
Climb the arête L of 14.55, then move L on to the wall and over
the O/H. Hand-TR R into a shallow groove until it is possible to
pull over.

** *14.55* **Black Hawk Bastion**   55 ft./17 m.   E2   (5c)
Ascend a steep groove with one awkward step below the O/H.
Move L in a spectacular swing to finish.

* *14.55A* **Eliminator**   50 ft./15 m.   HVS   (5b)
Climb the R arête of 14.56 and the discontinuous crack up the
steep wall above and R.

*** *14.56* **Black Hawk Slit**   80 ft./24 m.   S   (4a)
Layback the polished angle crack to a wider section, which is
jammed. It eases above.

** *14.57* **Black Hawk Traverse Left**   55 ft./17 m.   VD   (2c)
Climb the wall centre and TR L (crux) before moving up to a
large ledge behind a tower. Various finishes.

* *14.57A* **Providence**   50 ft./15 m.   E1   (5b)
Start as 14.57. Climb direct where it goes L, taking a thin crack,
steep wall to R and easier wall above.

** *14.58* **Blizzard Chimney**   80 ft./24 m.   D.   (2c)
A crack leads into the chimney and there is a stance below an
overhang above. Step L across the chimney and climb the main
wall.

** *14.59* **Gargoyle Buttress**   50 ft./15 m.   VS   (4b)
TR out from the R to a block above the O/H and climb the wall
above.

** *14.59A* **Dry Rot** 45 ft./14 m. E1 (5b)
Climb an o/ʜ on the ʀ of the buttress and continue up its ʀ edge.

** *14.60* **Manchester Buttress** 50 ft./15 m. S (4a)
The arête is climbed and a swing ʟ avoids the o/ʜ and allows a further ᴛʀ ʀ. An awkward pull round on to the arête follows before it eases.

** *14.61* **Crack and Corner** 45 ft./14 m. VD (3a)
Follow the V-groove throughout.

14.62 **Heather Wall** 45 ft./14 m. S (4a)
The steep wall is polished and reserves its crux to the upper reaches.

14.63 **Grotto Slab** 20 ft./6 m. M (1c)
The blocky slab is climbed from its lowest point. It can be escaped on the ʀ.

14.64 **Chimp's Corner and Grotto Wall** 55 ft./17 m.
VS (4c)
The overhung groove in the back of the Grotto is ascended with difficulty. From the ledge above, a scoop on the steep wall on the ʀ is reached and followed delicately to rounded ledges below the top (unprotected).

Burbage Edge

This fine escarpment lies along the east rim of the upper Burbage valley in a romantic and beautiful setting. Two miles in length, the edge is split into northern and southern sections by a subsidiary stream of Burbage Brook. It is readily reached from the Fox House Inn, all parts of the edge being within three-quarters of an hour's walk. Though popular, it is rarely as overcrowded as the southern end of Stanage.

Burbage North – Holly Ash Wall Area
(OS Ref 268822)

15.1 **Sentinel**   30 ft./9 m.   E2   (5c)
Ascend the front of the narrow block.

15.1A **Green Crack**   40 ft./12 m.   VD   (3a)
The crack is block-filled – climb it awkwardly.

** 15.2 **Holly Ash Crack**   45 ft./14 m.   VS   (4b)
The crack is wide and requires care, with knee-wedging moves at mid-height.

** 15.3 **Knight's Move**   45 ft./14 m.   VS   (4c)
Climb a shallow flake a few feet R of the crack. The bulge requires a long reach and it is then possible to finish direct or diagonally R. A lower TR R to 15.4 is a further alternative.

* 15.4 **Great Crack**   40 ft./12 m.   VS   (5a)
Move easily up the O/H and TR to the edge. Pull round the end and climb a shallow crack.

15.5 **Big Chimney Arête**   40 ft./12 m.   S   (3c)
After a pull over an initial O/H, climb the arête, with a mantelshelf at mid-height.

Burbage North – Obscenity Area   (OS Ref 269820)

16.1 **Brook's Layback**   25 ft./8 m.   S   (4a)
Jam and/or layback the crack.

16.2 **Wobblestone Crack**   25 ft./8 m.   VD   (3a)
A steep crack with alarming, but apparently safe, chockstones.

16.3 **Holly Bush Gully**   25 ft./8 m.   D   (2c)
The square gully.

** 16.4 **Obscenity**   40 ft./12 m.   VS   (4c)
After a steep start, climb the chimney to the O/H, using jams and awkwardly distributed holds to overcome it.

15   opposite above: *Burbage North, Holly Ash Wall*
16   opposite below: *Burbage North, Obscenity Area*

** *16.5* **Amazon Crack**   35 ft./11 m.   VS   (4b)
A beautiful straight jamming crack.

* *16.6* **Long Tall Sally**   30 ft./9 m.   E1   (5b)
The initial bulge is peculiar, while the groove above gives the crux.

* *16.7* **Greeny Crack**   30 ft./9 m.   VS   (4b)
The corner is straightforward, until the steep final moves to good holds on the R.

16.8 **Left Studio Climb**   30 ft./9 m.   VD   (3b)
Up the thin crack to the grassy bay. Climb the arête on the R and escape up the crack.

Burbage South – The Keep Area   (OS Ref 268813)

17.1 **Roof Route**   25 ft./8 m.   VS   (4c)
The crack is wide and forever awkward.

17.2 **Lethargic Arête**   25 ft./8 m.   S   (3c)
The slab on the L arête is climbed using a thin crack to the ledge and an easier arête above.

** *17.3* **Tower Climb**   40 ft./12 m.   S   (3c)
Pleasant cracks lead to the ledge. The chimney is escaped via a crack on the R wall after 10 ft./3 m. The curving crack on the L of the lower section gives Charlie's variant (vs, 4c)

17.4 **Tower Crack**   40 ft./12 m.   HVS   (5a)
Up the crack to the ledge. Finish by the overhanging layback above.

** *17.5* **The Boggart**   40 ft./12 m.   E2   (6a)
Start below the R-hand crack. Climb to a horizontal crack with difficulty. Move L and ascend the upper crack.

15.1   *The Sentinel, Burbage North. Andy Parkin*

***17.6 **Brook's Crack**   45 ft./14 m.   VS   (5a)
The initial steep crack is climbed until an awkward move into
the cave. Escape using the wide hand-jams.

***17.7 **Byne's Crack**   45 ft./14 m.   VS   (4b)
The crack provides excellent jams to a midway niche. The final
o/H can be outwitted by jamming and bridging tactics.

*17.7A **The Knock**   35 ft./11 m.   E4   (5c)
The R arête of the buttress.

Burbage South – The Quarries Area   (OS Ref 264809)

***18.1 **Pebble Mill**   35 ft./11 m.   E4   (6b)
Start on the R side of the buttress. Climb the R-hand arête to a
break (crux) and continue to the top.

18.1A **Above and Beyond the Kinaesthetic Barrier
25 ft./8 m.   E3   (6b)
Climb the L edge of the buttress.

*18.1B **Goliath**   25 ft./8 m.   E4   (6a)
A nose-grinding wide crack, most suitable for thin dwarfs.

18.2 **David   25 ft./8 m.   HVS   (4c)
A steep but elegant layback.

18.3 **Saul**   40 ft./12 m.   VS   (4c)
Up the wall, moving R to a mantelshelf, before finishing up
steep cracks on the L.

18.3A **Zeus**   45 ft./14 m.   E2   (5b)
Climb the steep crack (1PR)

18.4 **Hades**   40 ft./12 m.   HVS   (5b)
The corner is often damp. Poor jams lead to a hard mantelshelf
just above mid-height.

17   opposite above: *Burbage South, Keep Area*
18   opposite below: *Burbage South, The Quarries*

18.5 Fox House Flake   45 ft./14 m.   VS   (4b)
The flake lies demolished on the quarry floor. Follow the fine, slanting jamming crack to a stance. The final few moves are steep on generally adequate holds.

*18.6 **Dunkley's Eliminate**   30 ft./9 m.   VS   (4c)
Climb the L edge of the terraced wall, by a short problem and an exposed arête above.

18.7 **Millwheel Wall   30 ft./9m.   E1   (5b)
Reach the ledge below the green wall. Ascend it delicately, moving from L to R, with a slight easing in the upper sections.

18.8 **Scoop Crack**   40 ft./12 m.   S   (4b)
Climb a corner crack to the ledge. The groove is awkward for about 15 ft./4 m., when a move R leads to easier ground.

18.9 **Old Bailey   45 ft./14 m.   HVS   (5b)
A detached pillar is climbed by a crack on its L. The corner above is the crux.

*18.10 **Dover and Ellis' Chimney**   50 ft./15 m.   E1   (5b)
The deep groove is climbed with difficulty to a ledge. The chimney requires painful arm-wedging techniques to effect entry.

18.10A **Silent Spring   85 ft./26 m.   E4   (5c, 5c)
A traverse of the Cioch, just above its lip. Move on to the face from the L and reach a stance (bolts and P). TR to a flake, move downward R and finish L of the arête.

18.7   Millwheel Wall, Burbage South. Kim Carrigan

Higgar Tor   (OS Ref 255819)
The prominent leaning block of Higgar Tor is both a notable
landmark and a crag of remarkably distilled technical difficulty.
Two miles east of Hathersage and one and a half miles north-west
of Fox House, and within easy reach of the Ringinglow Road, it is
easily approached. The gritstone is of unparalleled roughness.

19.1–3   The four short cracks are all of deceptive steepness and
difficulty (4b–4c).

*** 19.4   **The Rasp**   55 ft./17 m.   E1   (5c)
Layback the steep flake to a semi-resting position where it widens.
Pull out R to the base of a shallow groove (thread) and climb it
with difficulty to a niche under the final O/H. Make a chin-grinding
TR R to escape.

19.5   **Surform**   45 ft./14 m.   HVS   (5a)
Climb 19.4 for 30 ft./9 m., but move L to a sloping ledge. Bulging
ledges provide easier climbing above.

** 19.6   **The File**   40 ft./12 m.   VS   (4c)
The crack is jammed in classic fashion.

19.7   **The Flute of Hope**   65 ft./20 m.   E3   (5c)
Climb 19.6 for 15 ft./4 m. and TR L on to the overhanging face to
below a steep crack. Reach 19.4 below the crux. Climb it to the
final niche and escape L with difficulty. The crack can also be
reached from below, via a small arête.

19.8   **Bat Out of Hell**   50 ft./15 m.   E5   (6a)
Climb an arête directly below the crack of 19.7. Go up a
vertical crack above, finishing at the same point as 19.4.

19   Higgar Tor

Millstone Edge   (OS Ref 248803)

The quarried walls of Millstone Edge and Lawrencefield only developed as climbing grounds during the last 35 years, unlike the majority of the natural gritstone crags. At first pitons were over-enthusiastically used, but the edges are now a major free-climbing ground where few pitons are necessary. Situated in a prominent and fine situation, overlooking the A625 two miles from Hathersage on the road to Fox House, the cliffs are easily approached in less than 15 minutes from the road.

The climbs are larger than the average gritstone, and piton belays are sometimes needed, while the rock is sometimes loose, especially near the top. There have been at least two climbing fatalities here in recent years, attributable to the looseness, but with care it should not deter competent parties, for it is far less than is accepted on many cliffs in modern climbing. The cliff is moderately popular, though rarely crowded.

Millstone Edge – Sandstone Cave Area

The first large bay beyond minor outcroppings boasts a 70 ft./21 m. wall with prominent sandstone caves.

20.1 **Oriel**   55 ft./17 m.   VS   (4c)
A thin crack leads to the R-hand cave. Step R on to the slab and ascend the slab direct.

20.2* **Gimcrack   70 ft./21 m.   VS   (4c)
The thin crack just L of the cave leads into a corner which eases beyond the o/H into easier slabby ledges and a loose finish.

20.3 **Shaftesbury Avenue**   70 ft./21 m.   HVS   (5a)
Climb the steep jamming crack to the o/H and continue with less difficulty.

***20.4* **Regent Street**   70 ft./21 m.   E2   (5c)
Follow the scarred crack, passing a bulge with difficulty, to reach an easier angled slab. Move R and climb the upper crack with shades of routes to come.

20   Millstone Edge, Sandstone Bay

20.5 **Jermyn Street   80 ft./24 m.   E4   (6a)
Start 10 ft./3 m. L of 20.4 up a thin crack. Climb it to the
Keyhole Cave. Move R to the lip and on to the wall above.
Move L and climb a peg scarred crack direct.

***20.6 **Coventry Street**   80 ft./24 m.   E4   (6b, 6a)
Climb direct to middle of cave and over roof after belay on L.

20.6A **Oxford Street   70 ft./21 m.   E3   (5b, 6a)
Jam the crack to the cave. Overcome the o/h (crux) and
continue up a finger crack.

20.7 **Skywalk**   85 ft./26 m.   S   (4a)
The corner is climbed to a large ledge and belay 30 ft./9 m.
from the top. A delicate and friable TR across the R wall is
undertaken until a direct finish is possible above the central
sandstone caves.

20.8 **Brixton Road**   90 ft./27 m.   D   (2b)
Climb the large crack to a TR at 50 ft./15 m. (possible belay).
TR L and climb the corner above.

20.9 **Petticoat Lane**   90 ft./27 m.   HVS   (4c)
Follow a thin crack up the centre of the wall to a fault. TR L 15
ft./4 m. and move up (PR) to the R to a narrow ledge. Finish on
poor holds.

21.1 **Lambeth Chimney   70 ft./21 m.   S   (4a)
A chimney L of the arête leads to a ledge (possibly PB). Up the
steep arête and step delicately into the upper chimney on the L,
to finish direct.

***21.2 **London Wall**   70 ft./21 m.   E5   (6a)
Follow the peg-scarred crack all the way.

***21.3 **The Mall**   70 ft./21 m.   VS   (4c)
Climb the diedre, which is steep and sustained.

21A   Millstone Embankment

***21.4 **Great Portland Street**   70 ft./21 m.   HVS   (5a)
Enter the corner by a mantelshelf. Follow the groove by
magnificent wide bridging.

***21.5 **Bond Street**   70 ft./21 m.   HVS   (5a)
Climb the sustained hand-jam crack to a niche. Leave this,
with difficulty, via a thin crack.

21.6 **Covent Garden   120 ft./36 m.   VS   (4b)
Ascend easy ledges to a steep mantelshelf on the L and climb
the arête to a large ledge R of the arête, or follow cracks on the R
to the same ledge. Climb the arête on the L, with a slightly
friable finish.

21.7 **Whitehall   100 ft./30 m.   HVS   (5a)
The lower corner is climbed, with some difficulty, to a large
ledge. The upper corner gives thin fingery climbing.

***21.8 **Time for Tea**   60 ft./18 m.   E2   (5b/c)
Climb the crack to its top. Move L and finish direct (5c), or TR
R to join another crack and climb it.

*21.9 **Embankment Route 3**   50 ft./15 m.   E1   (5b)
A thin crack leads L to the terrace.

*21.9A **Scritto's Republic**   50 ft./15 m.   E6   (6c)
A series of peg marks are followed. An ancient bolt runner.

21.10 **Embankment Route 2**   100 ft./30 m.   VS   (4c, 4c)
The prominent jagged-edged jamming crack leads to the
terraces. Finish by a prominent layback with a loose finish, or
by a thin once-pegged crack on the face (HVS, 5b).

21.10B **Technical Master**   100 ft./30 m.   E2   (5a, 5b)
Climb the ledge with difficulty to the terrace. Climb the wall L
of 21.10.

21B   Millstone Edge, Great North Road Area

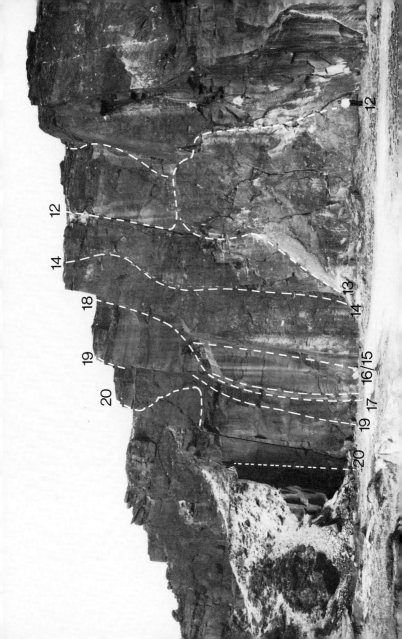

21.11 **Great North Road 110 ft./33 m. HVS (5a)
Up the slab and crack until a step R leads to the corner.
Layback the wedge-encumbered crack to a good stance (PB).
Climb the magnificent corner above, passing the roof, to an
easier groove.

*21.12 **Bypass** 120 ft./36 m. VS (4b)
Start up the crack of 21.11 and follow it past poised blocks to a
large terrace (belay). Finish up the brittle crack in the L back
wall of the terrace to a loose finish.

21.13 **The Scoop 120 ft./36 m. D (2b)
A long ramp, with good holds, leads into a groove and to the
terrace. The back corner of the terrace is best climbed on the R
and is most awkward to start and at the top.

***21.14 **Knightsbridge** 125 ft./38 m. E2 (5c)
Climb a steep corner to a large ledge and finish up the wall via
the thin crack.

*21.15 **Great Arête** 120 ft./36 m. E4 (5c, 6a)
As for 21.10 to the PR. Pendule R to the arête and go up to a
stance. Climb the continuation arête (crux) to the top.

***21.15A **Master's Edge** 60 ft./18 m. E7 (6c)
Climb the lower arête direct to 21.15 (1 Amigo, 1 Tricam,
pro.).

21.16 **Green Death** 120 ft./36 m. E5 (5c)
The blank corner is climbed with difficulty, particularly above
mid-height. (A PR was placed here on the first ascent by abseil.)
Finish up the corner above the large ledge.

21.17 **Edge Lane** 120 ft./36 m. E5 (5c)
Take the L arête of 21.16 to the terrace (2 PR placed by abseil on
first ascent). The upper arête has one bolt runner and is
climbed on the R.

21.18 **Great West Road** 130 ft./40 m. E1 (5b)
Climb the lower corner to the O/H and continue up the flake to
the terrace. Finish up the upper corner behind the ledge.

***_21.19_ **Xanadu**   130 ft./40 m.   E2   (5c)

Ascend the shot holes to the glacis and climb up to the corner, moving up to a ledge and PB. Climb the thin crack in the groove to a ledge 15 ft./4 m. from the top. Hand-TR spectacularly R to a steep finish.

_21.20_ **Crewcut – Myolympus   120 ft./36 m. HVS   (4c, 5b)

Take the layback direct, the last moves being the least secure. Move along the large ledge and up the flake 10 ft./3 m. L of the corner (21.19). Mantelshelf and climb the crack to a ledge, move L and finish by a hard move on the arête.

_21.20A_ **Stone Dri**   E2   (6a)

Take the corner direct.

Millstone Edge – Lyons Corner House Area

_22.1_ **Flapjack**   75 ft./23 m.   S   (3c)

A shallow corner just L of the square-cut buttress is climbed to a move R and mantelshelf on to a ledge. The groove above leads to an upper ledge. Finish up a thin crack.

_22.2_ **Diamond Groove**   95 ft./29 m.   HVS   (5b)

Follow a thin flake crack to a ledge on the R. Up to another ledge below the groove. Climb the groove delicately to a stance. Climb the short steep wall on good small holds.

_22.3_ **Pinstone Street   90 ft./27 m.   E2   (5c)

Climb the groove to the O/H (PR). Pass this, with difficulty, to a stance. Finish above on the R.

_22.4_ **Lubric   100 ft./30 m.   HVS   (5b)

The shallow groove leads into the cave (belay). Exit R steeply and climb somewhat dusty rocks to the base of a smooth corner. Climb the corner with considerable difficulty.

***_22.5_ **Twikker**   95 ft./29 m.   E3   (5c)

Climb the obvious peg-scarred crack out of the cave, over two bulges, to a smooth slab. Moving R at the first bulge reduces the standard.

22.6 **Lyons Corner House** 120 ft./36 m. HVS (5a)

Attain the cave (belay). Exit via the groove on the L and an exposed swinging TR to an awkward move on to a stance. Move steeply up the wall and step L to complete the route on a fine arête.

22.7 **Direct Start** 55 ft./17 m. VS (4c)

Follows a thin rib to the second stance.

Millstone Edge – Great Slab Area

*23.1 **Lorica** 80 ft./24 m. VS (4c)

A thin crack at the R end of the slab is followed to the thin flake. Layback the flake, with difficulty, to a ledge. Up the shallow corner to finish.

23.1A **Sex Dwarfs** 60 ft./18 m. E5 (6b)

Climb the slab 6 ft./2 m. R of 23.2.

23.2 **Great Slab 90 ft./27 m. S (4a)

The centre of the slab is climbed, avoiding moronic chisellings to the L, to a small ledge and belay. Up the crack, move R and finish up an easy friable chimney.

23.2A **The Snivelling 50 ft./15 m. E5 (6b)

Climb the smooth slab on minute rugosities to a hole, and finish direct.

23.3 **Svelt 65 ft./20 m. HVS (5a)

Delicate moves up the L corner of the slab lead to a stance (PB). Finish up the steep groove on the L.

Millstone Edge – Cioch Area

24.1 **Eartha 55 ft./17 m. S (4a)

Climb delicately to a ledge at 20 ft./6 m. Follow a thin flake up the slab centre.

24.2 **Cornerstone Climb**   55 ft./17 m.   S   (3c)
Take the R edge of the slab and keep R above. It is possible to
start up the L corner (4a).

24.3 **Close Shave**   90 ft./27 m.   S   (3c)
The cracks R of the upstanding block lead to its top. Follow the
corner above to finish.

*24.3A **Supra Direct**   60 ft./18 m.   HVS   (5b)
Takes the peg-marked crack direct and a thin crack above L.

*24.4 **Cioch Corner**   65 ft./20 m.   S   (3c)
The groove L of the Cioch is followed to a ledge. Finish up the
arête on the R.

***24.5 **Dexterity and April Arête**   100 ft./30 m.
HVS   (5b, 4c)
The fierce crack is climbed, with a hard move, to reach an
undercut flake. Move L with difficulty to the ledge (belay).
Climb the arête on the L delicately.

*24.5A **Dextrous Hare**   45 ft./14 m.   E3   (5c)
Follow scars, with difficulty, to a move L to the final flake.

*24.6 **March Hare**   35 ft./11 m.   HVS   (5b)
Take the lower arête direct.

Millstone Edge – North Bay

25.1 **Soho Sally   80 ft./24 m.   HVS   (5b)
Take a short steep crack to a pedestal stance, just L of the
shattered chimney. Climb the steep groove on the L, with
difficulty.

***25.2 **Saville Street**   85 ft./26 m.   E3   (5c)
Take the central crack direct all the way, passing an O/H at
two-thirds height.

25   Millstone Edge, North Bay

*25.3 **Remembrance Day**   70 ft./21 m.   VS   (4c)
A steep crack in the L corner of the bay leads to a stance. The finish remains awkward.

***25.4 **Plexity**   65 ft./20 m.   HVS   (5a)
The lower steep crack is sustained, leading to a shelf which allows an escape to belay in 25.3. Move L and climb the steep thin crack.

25.4A **London Pride   80 ft./24 m.   E3   (5c)
Climb a thin crack past O/H and move R (PR). Climb R and up to the O/H, finishing by a crack.

*25.5 **Estremo**   55 ft./17 m.   HVS   (5a)
Follow the wide s-crack, by difficult jamming, to the O/H and layback the steep corner above, passing loose blocks.

*25.6 **Hacklespur**   50 ft./15 m.   HVS   (5b)
The v-chimney groove is climbed by insecure back-and-foot techniques, changing direction at several points. Some of the holds are loose.

25.7 **Gates of Mordor   50 ft./15 m.   E3   (5c)
Ascend the groove and move L to a steep finishing crack.

25.8 **Satan's Slit**   45 ft./14 m.   HVS   (5b)
Awkwardly spaced holds lead to a move R into the crack proper. Climb it, with difficulty, to the niche, and less difficulty thereafter.

Lawrencefield   (OS Ref 249799)
The quarry is a hole in the ground, with an evil pond below the highest point. Its sheltered position is useful in chilly conditions, but encourages the midges on summer evenings.

26.1 **Three Tree Climb**   90 ft./27 m.   S   (4b)
TR a ledge to a tree and climb the groove delicately to reach a pedestal. Step R and climb the edge to a ledge and tree belay. Move L to escape.

**26.2 Pulpit Groove   90 ft./27 m.   VD   (3a)

Pull up a short wall into the base of the slanting groove and to up to the semi-detached block (belay). Tʀ the scoop ʀ to a ledge.

**26.3 Great Harry   80 ft./24 m.   VS   (4c)

Layback and jam the brown corner to the semi-detached block belay. Ascend a weird chimney to a step ʟ of the tree of 26.1. Finish direct on steep rock.

26.4 Scoop Connection   80 ft./24 m.   E2   (5b)

The wall is climbed to its ʀ edge. Make a steep move up ʟ and climb the scoop to rejoin 26.2 at the upper ledge.

*26.5 Suspense   80 ft./24 m.   E2   (5c)

As above to the ʀ-edge ledge. Climb the wall above the pool.

26.6 Lawrencefield Ordinary   80 ft./24 m.   VD   (3a)

Tʀ the ledges behind the pool to their ʟ extremity. Follow short corners to a large ledge. The steep wall is Tʀ ʟ to the big shelf above 26.5 (tree belay). Finish up shelving slabby rocks.

26.7 Austin's Flake   35 ft./11 m.   VS   (4c)

The layback flake above and ʀ of 26.6.

**26.8 SAE   80 ft./24 m.   HVS   (5b)

Follow 26.6 to where it traverses ʟ. Move ʀ to a sloping ledge. Climb the awkward corner to a mantelshelf and move ʀ up steep loose rock to finish.

**26.9 Boulevard   70 ft./21 m.   E3   (6a)

From the ʟ corner of the great shelf, climb the old peg crack direct.

***26.10 Billy Whizz   70 ft./21 m.   E2   (5c)

Climb the shallow groove in the middle of the wall, passing a ᴘʀ on the upper Tʀ, to reach a poor ᴘʀ below the steep wall. Move up to the slanting crack, climb it and the wall above.

26.9   *Pete O'Donovan on Boulevard, Lawrencefield*

**26.11 High Street   70 ft./21 m.   E3   (6a)
Follow the R-hand piton cracks with difficulty.

***26.12 Excalibur   80 ft./24 m.   VS   (4c)
Take easy rocks to a shelf on the R below the steep corner crack
(PB). Jam and layback the crack.

26.13 Jughandle   60 ft./18 m.   VD   (3a)
Ascend shelves above the R corner of the pool until a final steep
move to a ledge. Escape on the R (other finishes are harder).

*27.1 Limpopo Groove   35 ft./11 m.   VS   (4b)
Steep climbing up the groove with a hard exit.

*27.2 Gingerbread   30 ft./9 m.   VS   (4b)
Climb the edge delicately.

*27.3 Meringue   30 ft./9 m.   (4c)
Take the slab direct, the last move being the hardest.

*27.4 Snail Crack   50 ft./15 m.   HVD   (3b)
A thin crack gives interesting climbing.

*27.5 Stonemason's Climb   80 ft./24 m.   S   (4a)
Climb the ledges to a steep mantelshelf move and easier rock to
a belay. Move R and finish up a corner crack. Several
alternatives are offered above.

27.6 Blacksmith's Climb   70 ft./21 m.   VS   (4c)
Ascend the outleaning corner to a sloping ledge (crux) and pull
on to higher ledges. Finish up the wall on the L.

**27.7 Red Wall   60 ft./18 m.   HVS   (5a)
Ascend the wall, moving R to a small V-groove and ledge.
Mantelshelf up the wall with difficulty.

27.8 Delectable Variation   (4c)
TR the wall on the L to the arête, and climb it. This TR can be
reached direct by a thin crack and a direct finish is also possible
(HVS, 5b).

27.7   *Lawrencefield, Red Wall*

**27.9 Cordite Crack   50 ft./15 m.   S   (4b)
Sloping shelves lead into the corner, which is climbed by
layback.

Yarncliffe Quarry   (OS Ref 256795)

28.1 **Ants Arête**   55 ft./17 m.   S   (4a)
Climb the arête.

28.2 **Ants Wall**   55 ft./17 m.   S   (4a)
Take the crack containing a beech tree. Step R above it.

**28.3 Cardinals Crack   65 ft./20 m.   VS   (4b)
Climbed by wide hand-jams to the tree and a loose finish.

**28.5 Fall Pipe   60 ft./18 m.   VS   (4c)
Ascend the fierce crack with difficulty.

***28.5 Crème de la Crème   60 ft./18 m.   E4   (6b)
Climb the sharp arête direct (1 PR).

Yarncliffe Edge   (OS Ref SK256794)

*28.6 **Dicrotic**   60 ft./18 m.   VS   (4c)
Climb a steep wall to a ledge and a crack to the chimney above,
which has some loose rock.

*28.7 **High Heaven**   50 ft./15 m.   HVS   (5a)
A layaway crack leads by a birch to a glacis. Finish R by a
smooth short wall.

Tegness Pinnacle   (OS Ref 255777)

29.1 **Original Route**   30 ft./9 m.   D   (2b)
Climb the obvious stepped arête to the summit. (Descend the
same.)

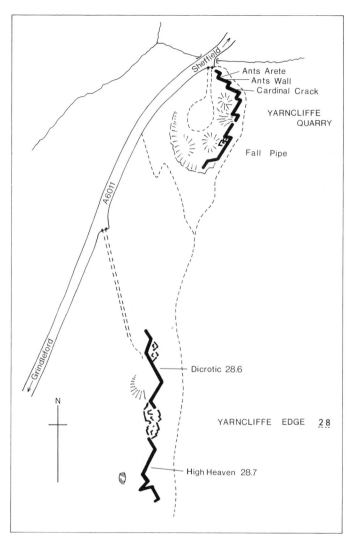

Sheffield

Ants Arete
Ants Wall
Cardinal Crack

YARNCLIFFE
QUARRY

Fall Pipe

A6011

Grindleford

N

Dicrotic 28.6

YARNCLIFFE   EDGE   <u>2 8</u>

High Heaven 28.7

29.2 **Pisa**   30 ft./9 m.   S   (4a)
Ascend a hard crack on the outer face of the pinnacle to a ledge,
follow this and finish via a short crack.

The Froggatt – Curbar – Baslow Edges

One of the finest of the eastern edges stretches for three miles
along the eastern edge of the Derwent valley. It is easily
reached from the track along the moor behind the edges, with
road access near the Grouse Inn (B6054) and at Curbar Gap.
   The gritstone is slightly less square-cut than the natural
edges of further north, and tends to be more lichenous.
Froggatt is very popular; the high standard of climbs of Curbar
and milder problems of Baslow Edge marginally less so.

Froggatt Edge   (OS Ref 250765)

30.1 **Strapiombante**   30 ft./9 m.   E1   (5b)
Up the arête to a crack, move up L and make a very hard move
to finish.

30.2 **Strapadictomy   35 ft./11 m.   E5   (6a)
Climb the arête on to the flake on the o/H. Finish up a steep
wall.

30.3 **Strapiombo**   30 ft./9 m.   HVS   (5b)
Climb to the o/H and jam out along the roof (good runner).
Swing round into a layaway position to overcome the o/H.

30.4 **North Climb**   40 ft./12 m.   VD   (3b)
The wide crack is awkward in the middle reaches.

***30.5 **Sunset Slab**   35 ft./11 m.   VS   (4b)
Move up into the scooped slab centre, step L and climb the
shallow groove to the top (unprotected).

***30.5A **Beau Geste**   40 ft./12 m.   E7   (6c)
The fine arête on the R is climbed past a small o/H to hard
moves on its L.

29   Tegness Pinnacle

Froggatt Area

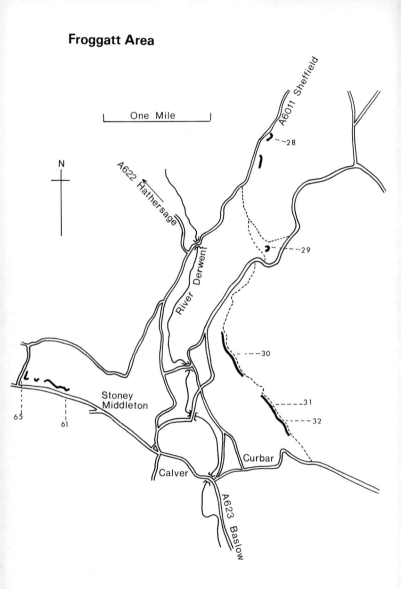

One Mile

N

A6011 Sheffield

A622 Hathersage

River Derwent

Stoney
Middleton

Calver

Curbar

A623 Baslow

—28

—29

—30

—31

—32

65

61

30.1   Strapiombante, Froggatt

*30.6 **Holly Groove**   30 ft./9 m.   HS   (4b)
Climb the steep corner, with some difficulty, past the tree.

30.7 **Hawk's Nest Crack   30 ft./9 m.   VS   (4b)
The crack is climbed with good jams, except for some awkward
moves at mid-height.

*30.8 **Cave Crack**   40 ft./12 m.   (5b)
Climb to the cave roof (runner). Tr out L with difficulty and
use jams to stand on the front face. Less difficult jamming
follows.

30.9 **Cave Wall   40 ft./12 m.   E3   (5c)
The o/H R of the cave is climbed, being at first strenuous then
delicate, to a mantelshelf and escape via the horizontal crack
(unprotected).

30.10 **Swimmer's Chimney   35 ft./11 m.   VD   (3a)
Back and foot until the chimney eases.

30.11 **Brightside   40 ft./12 m.   E2   (5c)
From 30.10, move R and climb the wall direct.

*30.12 **Terrace Crack**   40 ft./12 m.   S   (4a)
Climb the lower crack steeply. The upper section remains
awkward and sustained.

*30.13 **Heather Wall Variant**   70 ft./21 m.   HVS   (5a)
The cracks of 30.15 are followed to below the final crack. Tr L
to the edge and swing into a steep narrow crack which
gradually eases in ascent.

30.14 **Heather Slab**   55 ft./17 m.   E1   (5b)
Pull over the bulge just L of the cracks of 30.15. Climb the slab,
keeping R, passing 30.13's TR *en route* – poorly protected.

***30.15 **Heather Wall**   55 ft./17 m.   S   (3c)
The lower section of the buttress is split by a thin crack – up
this to a ledge. Follow improving cracks on the R to a final
jamming crack.

30   Froggatt Edge

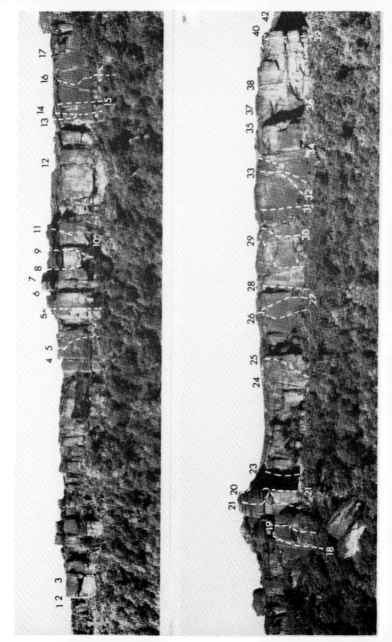

***30.16 **Tody's Wall**   60 ft./18 m.   HVS   (5a)
From the back of the bay, ascend to a projecting block
(runner). Stand on it and make an eccentric pull on to the slab.
Climb this and the thin crack to finish.

30.17 **Silver Crack**   30 ft./9 m.   S   (4a)
The wide awkward crack is followed throughout.

***30.18 **Three Pebble Slab**   35 ft./11 m.   HVS   (5a)
A slab leads to the bulge. Use a pocket to overcome this and
step up delicately on to the slab. Go up direct or step L before
climbing to the top. The pebbles have long gone (unprotected).

30.19 **Grey Slab**   35 ft./11 m.   S   (3b)
Up the slab, then move up R, with some difficulty, to a ledge.
The crack above offers a few holds.

***30.20 **Valkyrie**   65 ft./20 m.   HVS   (5a)
The steep crack is jammed on the ledge. Tr R to the stance on
the edge. Up R, then mantelshelf up on the L before easier
wrinkled climbing to the pinnacle top.

***30.21 **Narcissus and Narcissus II**   60 ft./18 m.
E6   (6b)
Climb the R arête to the stance of 30.18. Move L and climb a
shallow groove crack to the top.

*30.21A **Oedipus Ring Your Mother**   30 ft./9 m.
E4   (6b)
Make a hard Tr L across the wall and continue with difficulty to
a stance.

*30.22 **Chapman's Crack**   25 ft./8 m.   VS   (4a)
From the gully-top, Tr the gully wall of the pinnacle to a short
positive crack. Possibly the easiest route to the top.

30.23 **Diamond Crack   30 ft./9 m.   S   (4b)
The polished crack is steep and sustained.

30.21A   *Oedipus Ring your Mother*

30.24 **Broken Crack** 30 ft./9 m. VS (4b)
Layaway to start the crack and continue by steep positive jamming with little respite.

*30.25 **Sickle Buttress** 35 ft./11 m. S (3c)
Up the short crack to a slanting ramp. Follow this awkwardly to a final steep short wall.

*30.26 **Long John's Slab** 50 ft./15 m. E2 (5b)
Climb the centre of the slab to a flake and exit on the R. Unfortunately a vandalized route.

*30.27 **Downhill Racer** 50 ft./15 m. E4 (6a)
Go up diagonally L to a hard pull and straight up to finish.

30.28 **Slab Recess Direct** 60 ft./18 m. S (3c)
Climb the corner of the polished angle to a precarious exit. Finish by the easier flake above which can be reached from the R (D, 2c).

30.29 **Allen's Slab 55 ft./17 m. S (4a)
Move on to a ledge at 10 ft./3 m. and climb a diagonal break leading up R. Tr R delicately and finish up the wall just L of the crack.

30.30 **Trapeze 45 ft./14 m. VD (3b)
The cracks lead to a bulge. Move R and climb the edge via a groove. The direct exit is over the bulge (VS, 4b).

*30.31 **Heartless Hare** 40 ft./12 m. E5 (5c)
Climb the L side of 30.32, with a difficult section at two-thirds height. (Runner used on L originally – E3.)

***30.32 **Great Slab** 60 ft./18 m. E3 (5b)
From a ledge a few feet up, climb a delicate scoop to a point just R of a Tr ledge. Move R, with difficulty, to a second shelf and climb the still difficult steep wall above (unprotected).

***30.33 **Hareless Heart** 50 ft./15 m. E5 (5c)
Start R of 30.32 and climb to the Tr. Ascend the scoop above with difficulty (unprotected).

30.34 **Flake Gully** 30 ft./9 m. D (2c)
Follow the gully behind the R edge of the flake to its top, step across on to the wall and use a flake to finish on the L.

30.35 **Brown's Eliminate 45 ft./14 m. E2 (5b)
Climb the arête to good ledges (crux). From the L end of the ledges, move up on small holds until a semi-mantelshelf leads to easier ground (unprotected).

***30.36 **Green Gut** 40 ft./12 m. S (3c)
The corner is taken direct.

*30.37 **Pedestal Crack** 40 ft./12 m. VS (4c)
The steep lower crack leads to a flake. Layaway moves overcome the upper O/H.

***30.38 **Big Crack** 50 ft./15 m. E1 (5b)
Overcome the first 15 ft./4 m. on good holds. Steep moves on dubious holds are necessary to enter the crack, which is strenuous.

***30.39 **Chequer's Crack** 45 ft./14 m. HVS (5a)
An ankle-breaking short crack leads to a small ledge (crux). Jam the upper crack.

30.40 **Chequer's Buttress 40 ft./12 m. HVS (5a)
Climb a short groove, step out L on to the wall and TR diagonally towards the arête (runner). Make a long stretch for a good hold, above which the climbing eases. It is also possible to climb shallow cracks R of the edge all the way (5b).

30.41 **Solomon's Crack** 40 ft./12 m. VD (3a)
Up the obvious groove. Finish by either of two cracks.

*30.42 **Janker's Crack and Janker's Groove** 30 ft./ 9 m. VS (4 b/c)
The wide crack leads to a jutting block. Climb the crack above or move R to take the more awkward groove.

Curbar Edge – The North Section
The Deadbay (OS Ref 253757–255754)

**31.1 Deadbay Groove/Direct 40 ft./12 m. E2 (5b) or E3 (6a)
Enter the awkward groove and climb it on the o/h. Either move R to finish, or move L over the o/h and finish direct.

**31.2 Deadbay Crack 40 ft./12 m. E1 (5b)
Take the crack direct by jams and layaway at the crux at 25 ft./8 m.

*31.3 Cioch Left Hand 35 ft./11 m. VS (4c)
A steep awkward crack leads to the cave. Move on to its R wall and ascend until a steep step into the final crack.

31.4 Cioch Crack 40 ft./12 m. S (4a)
A crack on the R front of the buttress is climbed to a mantelshelf at 20 ft./6 m. Move L into a wide crack ending below the Cioch top. Move L and mantelshelf to finish.

31.5 Duggie's Dilemma 35 ft./11 m. VS (4b)
Layaway up the groove to below the final steepening and pull over by a chock crack.

31.6 Tree Wall 35 ft./11 m. HVS (5a)
A thin crack is followed throughout, with considerable difficulty just below the horizontal crack.

**31.7 Moon Walk 50 ft./15 m. E4 (6a)
The rounded L arête of the big split buttress is climbed on round holds. Serious.

31.8 Moon Crack 50 ft./15 m. E4 (6b)
The thin bulging crack R of the above is climbed to a break. Move R and finish more easily.

31.8 Moon Crack, Curbar. Martin Boysen

***31.9** **Sorrell's Sorrow**   40 ft./12 m.   VS(4c)
Take the steep crack by jamming with a bold move where it
widens. Above, the angle is less, but the moves are still
technical.

31.9A **Ulysses or Bust**   30 ft./9 m.   E5   (6b)
A hard modern arête.

31.9B **Soyuz**   35 ft./11 m.   E2   (5c)
Follow the flake to its end and finish direct or R.

31.10 **Apollo**   75 ft./23 m.   E2   (5b)
A short wall leads to a ledge. Move up and L and climb the
R-hand of the two cracks to a large ledge (belay). Move R
beneath the O/H until below the crack in the buttress. Reach the
crack, climb it and finish by difficult moves.

*31.11 **Two Pitch Route**   45 ft./14 m.   VS   (4c)
Take a short jamming crack until a step R leads into the gully.
Jam the elegant and unprotected upper crack.

***31.12** **The Brain**   60 ft./18 m.   VS   (4b)
Cross the slab by a foot-TR R above a hole. Go up to the ledges
on the R. Take the fine groove on the L, finishing on its L arête.

31.13 **Birthday Groove**   25 ft./8 m.   E1   (5c)
An isolated, ferocious short groove, higher on the hillside above
and to the R of 31.12.

Curbar Edge – The South Section   (OS Ref 259739)

32.1 **Avalanche Wall   50 ft./15 m.   HVS   (5a)
Thin cracks steepen to a bulge, where difficult steep moves are
the crux, moving on to dubious blocks.

***32.1A** **One Step Beyond**   60 ft./18 m.   E6   (6b)
Start as for 32.1 until a move R for a few feet. Go straight up to
a further move R across the wall to an easier finish. Serious.

31   opposite above: *Curbar Edge, Central Area*
32   opposite below: *Curbar Edge, Great Cracks Area (South)*

***32.2 **Owl Arête**   50 ft./15 m.   VS   (4c)
Go up a groove and swing L on to the delicate arête. After a
steep move, it eases. On the R of the bay begins:

***32.3 **PMC 1**   50 ft./15 m.   VS   (4b)
Fine twin cracks are followed to a ledge. Ascend the wall by a
diagonal TR in excellent position.

***32.3A **Profit of Doom**   60 ft./18 m.   E4   (6b)
Start R of 32.3. TR R to a resting place on the arête. Enter the
hanging groove and climb it direct. It is also possible to climb
up the lower groove direct.

***32.4 **Elder Crack**   70 ft./21 m.   E2   (5b)
Up the blocks to a chimney. Wedge the leaning crack to a hold,
which is used to attain a standing position. Layback the mighty
fierce upper crack (poorly protected).

32.4A **Slab Route**   30 ft./9 m.   S   (4a)
Climb the quarried slab on awkwardly placed holds.

32.5 **Bel Ami   70 ft./21 m.   VS ⁻(4b)
An even-sided jamming crack leads to a terrace. An arête gives
a fine finish.From the same point begins:

32.6 **Green Crack   35 ft./11 m.   HVS   (5a)
Step R on to the leaning flake and move up to a runner.
Layaway round the edge to reach good holds in a sensational
position.

32.7 **Usurper   35 ft./11 m.   E4   (6a)
Climb the steep crack to the roof. Move L to a crack and climb
it. Move L again to finish on 32.6.

32.8 **Maupassant   30 ft./9 m.   HVS   (5a)
Climb the layback crack direct, passing the chock with
difficulty.

32.3A   *Profit of Doom. Nigel Baker*

32.9 L'Horla   30 ft./9 m.   E1   (5b)
Ascend the groove, move L over the o/н and finish
phlegmatically up the arête.

32.10 Insanity   30 ft./9 m.   E2   (5c)
Layback until there is little footspace in a very difficult final
move.

32.11 Left Eliminate   40 ft./12 m.   E1   (5c)
A most awkward jamming problem requiring resource and
technique.

32.12 Peapod   60 ft./18 m.   HVS   (5b)
Enter the Peapod steeply and back and foot facing L. After the
exit (crux), the crack remains steep, though well protected.

32.12A Shape of Things To Come   60 ft./18 m.
E5   (6a)
Climb the wall to a slot and up R to a ramp system which is
followed L to a horizontal. Move L then straight up to finish.
Serious.

32.13 Right Eliminate   60 ft./18 m.   E3   (5c)
Ascend the wide crack by arm and leg wedging, passing several
chockstones. Above the last of these, it is difficult to adhere or
progress.

32.13A Linden   60 ft./18 m.   E6   (6b)
Start from the flake. Move up L across a small slab. Ascend a
bulge and wall, moving slightly L then R and up to a ledge.
Finish direct. Serious.

32.14 Scroach   70 ft./21 m.   E3   (5c)
From a pedestal, move up a crack. At the top, move on to a
ledge on the R, TR L for 10 ft./3 m. and climb direct on good
holds, exiting by a ramp on the L.

32.15 Hercules   35 ft./11 m.   VS   (5a)
The strenuous steep wide crack on the R.

Beyond the Curbar gap, Baslow Edge has many short interesting climbs, but nothing of sufficient calibre for inclusion.

Gardoms Edge   (OS Ref 271732)

The mile-long edge overlooks the A621 two miles east of Baslow. Composed of irregular buttresses and bays of gritstone, its base is tree-shrouded. Perhaps for this reason the edge is more lichenous after rain than most of the eastern edges. It is approached in about 30 minutes from Baslow, while the north end of the edge touches the road. It is best to approach climbs by walking along the top.

33.1 **Black Wall Route 1**   35 ft./11 m.   VD   (3a)
Climb a short chimney. TR L to the corner and finish up smooth bulges.

***33*.1A **Sleeping Sickness**   35 ft./11 m.   E3   (5c)
From the platform of 33.2, climb a thin crack to the o/H. Move L and pull up the front of the tower to finish.

***33*.2 **Brown Crack**   60 ft./18 m.   VD   (3b)
Up to the platform. Climb the fine crack and chimney.

33.2A **The Rattle**   60 ft./18 m.   HVS   (5a)
Make a difficult mantelshelf and climb the buttress direct.

****33*.3 **Lightning Wall**   45 ft./14 m.   HVS   (5a)
From the gully, move on to a sloping shelf and TR R to the exposed edge. Climb it delicately.

33.4 **Vaya Con Dios**   60 ft./18 m.   E2   (5c)
Climb a short crack to the stomach-TR L. Follow this to a wide vertical crack (runner). Continue along the horizontal on to the buttress front and stand up precariously – above it eases.

33.4A **Spanish Fly**   55 ft./17 m.   E5   (6c)
Takes the roof of 33.4 direct.

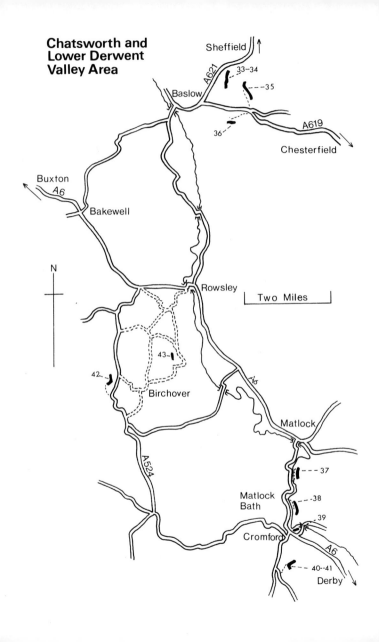

Chatsworth and Lower Derwent Valley Area

**33.5 Overhang Buttress 55 ft./17 m. S (3c)
As 33.5 to the vertical crack – climb it awkwardly.

33.6 Traction 35 ft./11 m. S (4b)
Over an o/ʜ to a jamming crack. Pull over the second o/ʜ direct to a ledge. Ascend the o/ʜ above or the arête to the ʀ.

33.7 Gardom's Gate 35 ft./11 m. VD (3a)
Ascend the chimney to an o/ʜ and ledge. Move ʟ (5 ft./2 m.) and climb the o/ʜ.

**33.8 Moyer's Climb 35 ft./11 m. S (3c)
The face is climbed centrally. A steep step ʀ is necessary to finish. (The ʟ exit is easier.)

*33.9 Nowanda 35 ft./11 m. HVS (5a)
Take the steep cracks to the base of the shallow jamming-crack. Ascend this with difficulty.

33.9A Landsick 35 ft./11 m. E3 (6a)
Climb the ʀ hand crack and finish direct. A move out ʀ reduces the standard to HVS (5a).

33.10 Garden Face Direct 50 ft./15 m. VS (4c)
Start on the ʟ of the buttress until the front face can be reached. Climb it direct.

*33.11 Heather Wall 40 ft./12 m. VD (3a)
Up the wall to a ledge. A thin crack leads to the roof and an exit ʀ.

**33.12 Och Aye Wall 40 ft./12 m. VS (5a)
A technically hard start on small holds leads to a ledge on the ʟ arête. Move ʀ up the upper face. One can avoid the ledge.

*33.13 Tartan Route 40 ft./12 m. VS (5a)
Long reaches lead to a midway ledge. Climb the upper wall slightly to the ʀ (unprotected).

33.14 Slime Crack 35 ft./11 m. VS (4b)
Jam the initial crack and overcome the upper choked crack.

33.15 **Green Crack**   35 ft./11 m.   S   (4a)
The first few feet are undercut. Layback and jam the upper section.

***33*.16 **Cave Arête**   60 ft./18 m.   HVS   (5a)
Ascend the cave back to a thread. Jam the o/ʜ with difficulty to a stance. The upper rib on the ʀ is delicate.

***33*.16A **Stormbringer**   65 ft./20 m.   E3   (5c)
Start from the cave of 33.16. Pull over the o/ʜ to a ledge and finish more or less direct.

****33*.17 **Moyer's Buttress**   65 ft./20 m.   E1   (5b)
The cracked slab leads to the o/ʜ. A bold swing on steep rock leeds on to the face, which is delicate, sustained and poorly protected.

***33*.17A **Biven's Crack/Variation**   65 ft./20 m.
E1/5   (5b)
Climb the overhanging crack to the horizontal and move ʀ to finish. Alternatively, climb the upper wall direct. (Perfect Day E5, 6b).

***33*.18 **Elliot's Buttress Indirect**   80 ft./24 m.
VS   (4b)
From 20 ft./6 m. up the ʟ gully, ᴛʀ the wall on the ʀ to the nose (ledge). Take the arête to finish.

****33*.19 **Eye of Faith**   80 ft./24 m.   HVS   (5b)
Climb a short overhung groove, move ʟ and layback a thin flake to a crack. Ascend the arête above by a series of sustained moves to the ledge. Finish as for 33.18.

****33*.20 **Elliott's Buttress Direct**   80 ft./24 m.   S   (3c)
A crack near the gully leads back to the gully edge. Climb a crack to the flake ledge. The final wall above is the crux.

33   opposite below: *Gardoms Edge South*
34   opposite above: *Gardoms Edge North*

33.21 **Dead Tree Wall**   60 ft./18 m.   VD   (3a)
TR the quarried wall from R to L, moving up to a ledge. Climb an awkward groove on the R edge of Elliott's Buttress.

34.1 **Undertaker's Buttress   70 ft./21 m.   VS   (4c)
A short crack is quitted on the R for a ledge. Ascend the awkward wall to a large ledge (thread belay). TR under the nose to the R and climb a crack with shelving holds.

*34.2 **Hearse Arête**   60 ft./18 m.   E1   (5b)
From the toe of the buttress, climb a scoop to the ledge and climb just R of 34.1 to the ledge (thread). Up a thin crack and overcome the O/H.

34.3 **Marshall's Route**   50 ft./15 m.   HVS   (5a)
Climb the wall R of the short crack and TR R to a good hold. Move up past a flake to a ledge, continue up the crack and exit L up the face.

34.4 **Stepped Crack**   50 ft./15 m.   D   (2b)
Follow the crack past a chockstone to a TR exit.

34.5 **Gardom's Unconquerable   50 ft./15 m.
VS   (4c)
Enter the crack by pulling awkwardly over the O/H. Layback and/or jam the upper crack. Finish up the wall behind.

34.5A **Whillans Blind Variant**   E1   (5b)
This makes a spectacular swing L from the flake belay.

34.6 **Tree Buttress**   40 ft./12 m.   VS   (4b)
A gully and rib lead to the tree on the ledge on the R. A fine crack is climbed by layback moves.

34.7 **Central Crack**   55 ft./17 m.   HVS   (5a)
Climb the wide crack, overcoming an O/H with difficulty, to belay below a corner. Bridge the corner more easily.

34.7A **Crocodile   35 ft./11 m.   E3   (5c)
Start round the arête from 34.7, below a thin crack in a steep wall. Climb it direct.

34.8 Capillary Crack   30 ft./9 m.   VS   (4b)
A rib leads to a thin crack and o/н with good holds.

34.9 Whisky Wall   40 ft./12 m.   VD   (3a)
From a ledge, move ʀ on to the face and ascend the arête
delicately.

**34.9A Waterloo Sunset   50 ft./15 m.   E3   (5c)
The obvious and unprotected arête to the ʀ. Easier high up.

**34.10 Finale Groove   50 ft./15 m.   HVS   (5a)
The initial moves lead to a bulge (first jams). Above this, there
remain awkward moves before a more definite crack.

*34.11 Babylon Groove   45 ft./14 m.   VS   (4c)
The groove is climbed taking the ʀ fork for a short distance
before moving ʟ and finishing up the wider groove.

*34.12 Tree Groove   40 ft./12 m.   VS   (4b)
This initial crack is climbed to a tree. Move ʀ and finish up a
deep crack.

34.13 Layback   30 ft./9 m.   VS   (4c)
The leaning crack is strenuous epsecially at the finish.

34.14 Flake Crack   50 ft./15 m.   S   (3c)
Leg and arm jam to the flake, pull round it and reach a ledge.
Above, there is a short difficult wall.

**34.15 NMC Crack   50 ft./15 m.   VD   (2c)
Climb the obvious flake to a ledge and final crack.

**34.16 Apple Arête   50 ft./15 m.   VS   (4c)
Attain the buttress from the ʀ and follow the edge by a series of
mantelshelf moves. Direct start: E4 (5c)

34.17 Apple Crack   50 ft./15 m.   D   (2b)
Climb the initial crack and an easy chimney.

*34.18 Cider   35 ft./11 m.   VS   (5a)
A delicate wall climb.

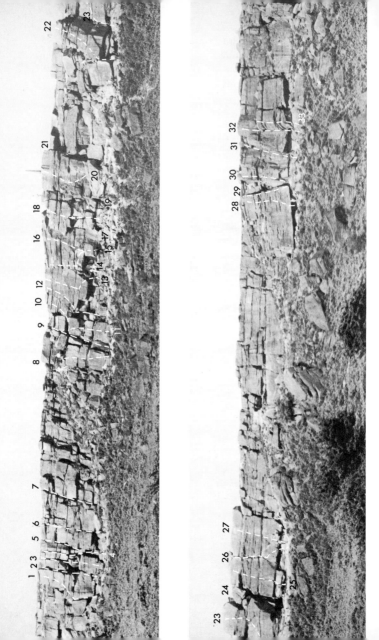

34.19 **Blenheim Buttress** 60 ft./18 m. VS (5a)
Mantelshelf up to reach the o/H, Move R and make difficult
moves up the upper buttress. Several hundred yards south is an
isolated tower.

*34.20 **Left-hand Pillar Crack** 35 ft./11 m. E1 (5b)
The crack is laybacked.

*34.21 **Right-hand Pillar Crack** 35 ft./11 m.
HVS (5a)
A technical jamming problem.

Birchens Edge (OS Ref 278728)
This compact gritstone edge lies east of Gardoms Edge, half a mile
from the A619 where it passes the Robin Hood Inn. Though it is a
beginner's crag, there are nevertheless fierce climbs of high quality.
The rock dries quite quickly after rain. Below, there is an excellent
campsite – ask permission at the farm.

35.1 **Crow's Nest 40 ft./12 m. VS (4c)
Climb the jamming-crack and move R on to the face as soon as
possible. Take the slab near its centre, the latter moves proving
difficult.

35.2 **The Funnel** 40 ft./12 m. D (2a)
Attain a platform at 20 ft./6 m. Back and foot the chimney.

35.3 **Kiss Me Hardy** 40 ft./12 m. VD (3b)
Climb a wall to a ledge. The wide crack is awkward.

35.4 **Victory Crack 45 ft./14 m. S (4a)
Pass a chockstone (35.5) and reach the ledge. Step L and jam
the steep crack.

35.5 **Victory Gully** 45 ft./14 m. S (4a)
Pass the chockstone and climb the upper crack with difficulty.

35 Birchens Edge

35.6 **Emma's Dilemma**   40 ft./12 m.   S   (4a)
Climb a steep initial crack, then progress more easily to a steep last move.

35.7 **Emma's Delusion**   40 ft./12 m.   VD   (3a)
Easy rock leads to a cave. Exit via a steep crack on the R and finish direct.

35.8 **Captain's Bunk**   55 ft./17 m.   S   (4b)
The slab is divided by two ledges. Mantelshelves are overcome in succession to a final steeper wall, taken via thin cracks.

35.9 **Telescope Tunnel**   45 ft./14 m.   M   (1c)
A deep gully is taken until it is possible to climb a crack and through route on the R to avoid the o/H.

***35.10 **Porthole Buttress**   80 ft./24 m.   VD   (2c)
Take the same route to the cave and follow an exposed shelf R to its end. Make a steep move on to the slab and exit direct on the R.

***35.11 **Porthole Direct**   50 ft./15 m.   S   (4b)
Difficult lower rocks lead to a v-groove, which is difficult to enter and leave. The overhanging crack is followed direct.

35.12 **Blind Eye**   50 ft./15 m.   S   (4a)
Climb the cave back and exit R on to 35.13, finishing by moving out to the R.

35.13 **Nelson's Slab   40 ft./12 m.   S   (4b)
Make difficult moves on the R edge of the slab and TR into its centre, continuing direct.

35.14 **Left Ladder Chimney**   40 ft./12 m.   D   (2b)
The lower half of the climb to a bulge is most difficult.

***35.15 **Sail Buttress**   45 ft./14 m.   S   (4a)
Mantelshelf on to a ledge and make further difficult moves L on to the arête, which is followed to the top. An entry from the L is VS (4c).

*35.16 **Ratline**   40 ft./12 m.   HVS   (5a)
Climb to the ledge and ascend the wall from its R edge. Move L
and over the bulge with difficulty, following the slab above
direct.

35.17 **Sail Chimney   45 ft./14 m.   HVD   (3a)
Enter the crack direct or from the R. Back and foot the upper
chimney.

***35.18 **Topsail**   40 ft./14 m.   VS   (4b)
Follow the flake crack to the o/Hs (thread). Pull over boldly on
to easier rock.

35.19 **Monument Chimney**   45 ft./14 m.   D   (2a)
Climb the back of the V facing R.

35.20 **Orpheus Wall**   45 ft./14 m.   HVS   (5b)
Make strenuous steep moves up the wall, going L to the bulge.
The pull-over is the crux.

35.21 **Monument Gully**   50 ft./15 m.   D   (2b)
Up the slab to the narrows. Back and foot to a ledge (belay).
Climb the slab on the L.

35.22 **The Chain   40 ft./12 m.   VD   (3b)
Escape from the corner on to the slab on the R and go up to a
ledge. TR R and ascend the buttress direct.

***35.23 **Powder Monkey Parade**   55 ft./17 m.
S   (4a)
Pull on to the easy section of Holly Bush Gully – TR R below the
o/H on to the slab. Climb this direct (unprotected).

35.24 **Admiral's Progress**   40 ft./12 m.   M   (1c)
Climb the chimney direct.

35.25 **Camperdown Crawl   40 ft./12 m.   S   (4a)
A thin overhanging crack leads to a ledge. The face above is
climbed direct with difficulty.

***35.26 **Trafalgar Crack**   45 ft./14 m.   VD`   (3a)
Reach the crack from the R, following a shelf. The crack is climbed direct. Somewhat unprotected.

35.27 **Trafalgar Wall   35 ft./11 m.   VD   (3b)
Climb the scratched face direct – unprotected.

35.28 **Copenhagen Wall**   30 ft./9 m.   MVS   (4b)
Move up with difficulty, then R and up to a final buttress, which is climbed direct.

35.29 **Mast Gully Ridge**   30 ft./9 m.   D   (2b)
The ridge is climbed direct.

35.30 **Mast Gully Buttress**   40 ft./12 m.   VS   (4b)
Move R on to the face from the gully. Climb it trending R.

35.31 **Fo'castle Chimney**   35 ft./11 m.   D   (2b)
The groove is taken direct.

35.32 **Cave Gully**   35 ft./11 m.   D   (2c)
The cave is climbed and left with difficulty.

35.33 **Tar's Arête**   35 ft./11 m.   D   (2c)
Pull over the bulge and continue more easily.

Chatsworth Edge   (OS Ref 275720)
This edge lies just south of the A619, two miles east of Baslow. It is a quiet, secluded place, though its northerly aspect tends to make the rock green after rain. The climbing is generally hard, in sharp contrast to nearby Birchens Edge. The approach takes only five minutes from the road.

36.1 **Strangler's Groove**   30 ft./9 m.   VD   (3a)
Climb the groove to the tree and finish on the R.

*36.2 **Throttled Groove**   25 ft./8 m.   S   (4a)
A steep layback corner.

*36*A   *Chatsworth Edge East*

36.3 **Choked Crack**   40 ft./12 m.   D   (2a)
The flake-filled crack.

*36.4 **Puppet Crack**   50 ft./15 m.   HVS   (5b)
The first moves of the leaning crack prove problematic.

***36.5 **Sentinel Crack**   55 ft./17 m.   E2   (5c)
Ascend into the recess, TR L and overcome the o/H by difficult jamming.

36.5A **Sentinel Buttress   70 ft./21 m.   E3   (5c)
Start as 36.5 to the roof. Move R to a rib and climb this to a break. Move L and finish just R of 36.4.

36.6 **Cave Climb   40 ft./12 m.   D   (2b)
Climb the wide crack and escape behind a chockstone.

*36.7 **Cave Crack**   40 ft./12 m.   S   (4a)
A wide crack proves difficult. Finish direct.

36.7A **Lichen   100 ft./30 m.   E2
1) 35 ft./11 m. (5a)   Start on the R of the buttress. Traverse into 35.7.
2) 35 ft./11 m. (5b)   Move L and hand-TR into the gully.
3) 40 ft./12 m. (5b)   Move L on the break and finish R of 36.5.

36.8 **High Step**   35 ft./11 m.   E1   (5b)
From the middle of the slab, climb L, making the step to reach a ledge. Step R to finish up a crack.

36.8A **Price**   30 ft./9 m.   HVS   (5a)
Start on R of wall. TR L to a niche and continue direct.

36.9 **Left Twin Crack**   40 ft./12 m.   S   (3c)
Follow the wide crack throughout.

***36.10 **Emerald Crack**   50 ft./15 m.   E2   (6a)
Take the steep crack direct to finish over the bulge.

*36*B   *Chatsworth Edge West*

***36.10A **Pearls**   40 ft./12 m.   E2   (5c)
: Start on the R wall of Emerald Buttress. Climb thin cracks and finish direct.

36.11 **Vibrio   45 ft./14 m.   E1   (5b)
: Ascend the crack to the o/H and pull over into the horizontal crack. Using a pocket, TR L with difficulty to finish up the arête. Direct from the pocket is harder (E3, 6a).

36.12 **Broken Buttress**   50 ft./15 m.   S   (4a)
: Move up L to a shallow groove, exit L and reach a stance. Finish up the nose above.

*36.13 **Emperor's Flake**   40 ft./12 m.   D   (2b)
: From the L edge of the buttress, go up and detour on to the L-hand face to a flake. Up this and an exposed and rounded nose to finish.

*36.14 **Emperor's Crack**   45 ft./14 m.   VS   (4b)
: The chimney crack is most awkward.

36.14A **Despot**   40 ft./12 m.   E1   (5b)
: Move L from 36.15, start and climb the wall above. Direct start: 6b.

36.15 **Empress Crack**   45 ft./14 m.   S   (4a)
: Up the crack to the flake, pass it on the L and finish direct. It is possible to avoid the flake.

*36.16 **Prince's Crack**   45 ft./14 m.   S   (4a)
: Exit L from a deep corner to a ledge. Jam the R crack above.

The Lower Derwent Valley

South of Baslow, the eastern gritstone outcrops frequently, but far less regularly, in small cliffs and occasional quarries as at Beeley (OS Ref 267666) and Stancliffe (OS Ref 329549). To the west, there are natural and quarried cliffs near Stanton Moor and particularly at Cratcliffe. Despite these outcroppings, there is less climbing hereabouts than to the north until the Derwent cuts through limestone south of Matlock, forming fine cliffs of large size with a wealth of steep and serious climbing. Beyond Cromford, the gritstone, now massive and bouldery, outcrops naturally at Black Rocks and is quarried widely.

Though explorations began on both rocks before 1900, 'grit' hogged climbers' attention until about 1950, when a gradual shift towards interest in the steep, large, loose limestone cliffs began. Today the limestone climbing here is both of greater extent and more overall significance than the traditional gritstone, though both provide excellent climbing.

Generally westward-facing, the cliffs usually dry quickly and give climbing throughout the year. Black Rocks is north-facing in part and can be slower drying; while High Tor is somewhat exposed to wilder weather.

Access

Regular bus services follow the A6 from south and north. All the cliffs described can be reached in less than 20 minutes from the road, with the exception of the outlying gritstone cliff at Cratcliffe.

Camping

Caves abound near the limestone cliffs. Their use should be undertaken carefully, as troglodyte-hunting is a favourite sport for local owners and the authorities. This applies the more forcibly to the various apparently under-utilized bandstands and lovers' hideyholes which are seemingly dedicated to other purposes than honest sleep.

High Tor (OS Ref 298590)

Beautifully situated in a commanding position above the A6, a mile south of Matlock, this cliff is one of the finest in Derbyshire. Composed of a fairly sound limestone, the cliff provides steep climbing in the modern idiom, most of it of a high order of difficulty.

37.1A **A6 E5 (6b)

   1) 120 ft./36 m. Start at L side of the obvious roof below a smooth white wall. Climb to a grassy ledge and climb a groove above, moving R across a broken wall and through an overlap. Continue to the horizontal. Move few feet R and pull over the bulge to enter a shallow groove. Climb the groove to the top and move slightly L to finish.

37.1B **Roadrunner** E6 (6c)

   1) 100 ft./30 m. Hand-TR the lip of O/H of 37.1 to centre of wall. Climb L and join 37.1A to finish.

37.1 **M1 E2 (5b)

   1) 50 ft./15 m. Overcome the first O/H and climb the crack to a shelf (PB).   2) 60 ft./18 m. TR L and climb the crack to the top (PR on TR).

37.2 **Entropy VS (2a, 4c)

   1) 20 ft./6 m. Ascend easily to a corner and ledge (PB).
   2) 80 ft./24 m. Pull round the O/H on the L. Layback the magnificent crack, overcoming a final O/H.

37.3 **Layby** HVS (3b, 5b)

   1) 30 ft./9 m. Up a corner and past blocks and ledges (PB under O/H).   2) 80 ft./24 m. Pull over the O/H on the L and move R to pass a second. Up the corner to its end. Move R to a ledge (PB). Step L and climb the groove (1 PR) to steep loose rock.

*37.4 **Lamplight** VS (4c, 4c)

   1) 70 ft./21 m. Climb the back of the v-depression awkwardly and make a layback move to a stance.   2) 50 ft./15 m. Layback the black crack.

***37.5 **Highlight** HVS (4b, 5a)

   1) 35 ft./11 m. A short groove leads to a loose block ledge (PB).   2) 115 ft./35 m. Climb the crack to a black O/H. Pass it with difficulty (2 PR) and continue to the roof. TR L and layback the final crack.

37.6 Skylight VS (4b, 4c)
1) 60 ft./18 m. Follow the cracks to the terrace (PB).
2) 80 ft./24 m. The crack above is jammed. Semi-back and foot the O/HS. The chimney above is easier.

***37.7 Castellan E5 (6b, 6a)
1) 80 ft./24 m. As 37.6 to the terrace. TR R to the cave.
2) 120 ft./36 m. Climb the roof and crack above free with difficulty to the hanging flakes. Belay.   3) 60 ft./18 m. Move R past a bulge to the easier final section.

**37.8 Laurin E3 (5c, 6a)
1) 75 ft./23 m. From the cave (above) move up and R to a groove. Climb this and step L to belay.   2) 65 ft./20 m. Go up to the O/H. Climb it (crux) and climb up L to finish.

***37.9 Delicatessen E1 (5b, 5b, 4c)
1) 100 ft./30 m. From the cave (above) TR R along the lower break to a ledge. Follow thin cracks for 20 ft./6 m., move out R and TR R to a small ledge belay.   2) 80 ft./24 m. TR R to the diedre of 37.15 and climb it to ledge.   3) 40 ft./12 m. TR R to a flake (PR) and climb up to finish.

**37.10 Nightmare of Brown Donkeys E3 (5c, 5c)
1) 90 ft./27 m. Follow 37.8 for 30 ft./9 m. to a groove. Climb this and either pendule to a stance (37.8), or descend lower to the same point. Belay.   2) 90 ft./27 m. Go up to the roof and TR L under it, finishing on good holds direct near 37.7.

**37.11 Lyme Cryme E3 (5c, 5c)
1) 75 ft./23 m. Start at a black groove. Climb it and move up L to a black bulge. Pull over and belay on ledge of 37.9.
2) 100 ft./30 m. Follow 37.8 for a few feet, then move up L to a flake ledge. Go straight up over a bulge and finish direct.

***37.12 **Robert Brown**   E3   (5c, 5b)
1)   100 ft./30 m. Start below the middle of the central face, at a groove behind a tree. Climb the groove and pull through the o/h slightly to the l. Move r to a crack and climb to belay.   2)   65 ft./20 m. Either (a) Climb the crack above and l of the belay. Move r and climb the wall on pockets to the o/h. Move l and finish by the tree. Or (b) Climb the flake on the r and finish as for 37.13.

***37.13 **Darius**   E1   (5b/c)
1)   30 ft./9 m. Climb an awkward groove and belay.   2)   130 ft./40 m. Attain the crack above by steep layaway moves and climb it. Move r and follow a second crack to a large hold. Move up r and follow a second crack to a large hold. Move up r and pull out of the flake line for a few feet, then tr l to the upper flake. Climb it to the top (bolt r). Either finish direct or to the l (easier).

***37.14 **Debauchery**   HVS   (3a, 5a, 5b)
1)   30 ft./9 m. Up easy rocks to a tree stance.   2)   80 ft./24 m. Tr l and go up diagonally l to a wall. Climb this and a flake, then move l to a bulge. Pull over to stance (as 37.12).   3)   70 ft./21 m. Step l and pull over a bulge. Move l to a steep flake and climb to a break. Tr l to a groove, climb up and finish up r to a small groove.

***37.15 **Original Route**   HVS   (3a, 5a, 4c)
1)   30 ft./9 m. Up easy rocks to a tree stance (as 37.14).   2)   80 ft./24 m. Tr l and ascend diagonally r to the groove. Climb the steep crack to a stance.   3)   40 ft./12 m. Tr r and make steep moves to finish.

*37.16 **Tales of Yankee Power**   90 ft./27 m.   E5   (6b)
From the tree belay (above) on 37.15 climb the thin crack on the r to a poor rest. Go up and r to a thread, then back l to the arête. Move up and r to an overlap (p) and finish direct.

37.14   *Debauchery High Tor. Chris Jackson and Jack Street*

***37.17 **Flaky Wall**   120 ft./36 m.   E4   (6a)
From the tree belay (above), climb into the groove of 37.15.
Move R along flakes and up on to the wall and into a groove
above. Follow the flakes R above all the way and finish direct.

37.18 **Supersonic   120 ft./36 m.   E4   (6a)
Climb up a wall to a shallow groove. Climb the groove and
move R. Continue up and move L to join 37.17. Climb this until
it goes R. Continue direct up a thin crack to its end, move L
then up R and finish direct (crux). From good ledge finish more
easily.

***37.19 **Bastille**   125 ft./38 m.   E5   (6c)
Start a few feet R of the groove of 37.18. Climb past two bolts
and enter the groove from the R (crux). Ascend the groove and
move L to a rest place. Go steeply up the wall, past good bolts,
until level with a niche on the R. Move L to join 37.17 or slightly
R and finish direct.

***37.20 **Decadence**   E4   (6a, 5c, 5c)
1) 80 ft./24 m. Start 20 ft./6 m. R of 37.19 below a pillar. Move
L and pull over a bulge (crux) and move L to a groove. Climb
the groove. TR L and step down to bolt belays on
37.19.   2) Go down L to 37.17 at the crux. Climb it and 37.18
until a vague traversing ramp leads to 37.16. Step L to 37.15
and climb it to belay.   3) Go down 10 ft./3 m. and go L to a
thread. Go L to 37.13, move up and L to join 37.12 and finish up
it.

37.21 **The Pillar**   E4   (3a, 6a/b)
1) 30 ft./9 m. Climb to tree belay.   2) 100 ft./30 m. Go up a
black groove to O/H. PR. Go L and up to second O/H. Make a
difficult move to gain 1 PR then pass bulge on R to finish
steeply. The direct is 6b.

Wildcat Tor   (OS Ref 297575)

Though less impressive than High Tor, Wildcat Tor gives interesting climbing of high quality. It is approached by a footbridge in Matlock Bath, which leads via a riverside footpath to the north end of the cliff. The cliff is tree-shrouded at its base, but identification is eased by the wall of Willersley Castle grounds, which marks the north end of the major section.

Just R of the wall in a bay is:

38.1   **Catacomb**   VS   (4a, 4c)
1) 30 ft./9 m. A short crack leads to the cave.   2) 70 ft./21 m. Step R, pull over the bulge (1 PR) and climb the slab above to a yew. Continue direct and finish by a groove on the L. A direct route from the cave is possible (1 PR, VS, 4c).

*38.2   **Catastrophe Grooves**   HVS   (4c, 5a)
1) 50 ft./15 m. Climb a crack and a groove. Reach a ledge on the L, TR R and go up to a stance (PB).   2) 60 ft./18 m. Up the groove on the L for 20 ft./6 m., step R (PR) and go up another groove. Escape via a groove on the R.

38.3   **Coyote Buttress**   HVS   (4c, 5a)
1) 40 ft./12 m. Take the steep wall to a stance.   2) 90 ft./27 m. Ascend a corner on the R to below the O/H. Move R and up L on to the buttress. Follow the L edge (1 PR) to finish via an overhanging crack.

38.4   **Coyote Crack (Derek's Dilemma)   VS   (4b, 4c)
1) 50 ft./15 m. Follow the lower steep crack and move R to belay.   2) 70 ft./21 m. Move L and climb the steep crack, jamming the steep section.

*38.5   **Broken Toe Groove**   VS   (4b, 4c)
1) 50 ft./15 m. A wide groove is reached and followed past an awkward block to an O/H.   2) 70 ft./21 m. Enter a groove on the L and follow it passing an O/H awkwardly below the fir tree.

38.6 **Cat's Eye**   S   (3c, 3a)
1) 70 ft./21 m. A curved crack leads to a groove and cave.   2) 50 ft./15 m. Take wide cracks and blocks R of the cave and finish up a steep wall.

38.7 **McPlumb Wall   VS   (4c, 4c)
1) 70 ft./21 m. The shallow corner leads to a stance (PB).   2) 50 ft./15 m. Take the steep wall centrally to below the bulge. TR R and escape just L.

38.8 **Cougar Cleft**   100 ft./30 m.   S   (3c)
From the gully, climb the chimney and move via its L wall into the upper section. Continue direct.

38.9 **Tiger Route I**   VS   (4c, 4c)
1) 70 ft./21 m. Take an easy crack to the top of a flake. Make a steep leftward TR and climb the groove near the L edge, finishing on the rib below a stance (PB).   2) 80 ft./24 m. Climb a crack L of the arête, reaching it via a deep chimney.

38.10 **Tiger Route II   VS   (4c, 4c)
1) 70 ft./21 m. As 38.9 to the belay (PB).   2) 80 ft./24 m. Go R up loose rock to a bulge. Move L below a bulge and finish spectacularly on the arête.

38.11 **Tiger Chimney**   VD   (3c, 3c)
1) 120 ft./36 m. Go easily into the chimney and ascend inside it.   2) 20 ft./6 m. Exit R and avoid the loose rock to the L.

38.12 **Cat Walk**   VS   (3c, 4c, 3c)
1) 30 ft./9 m. Scramble up to flakes and climb a groove to a slope. Belay on a flake.   2) 60 ft./18 m. Step L and climb the groove (15 ft./4 m.). Move L and go up to a stance (PR). Exit via a short corner crack.

38.12A **Golden Yardstick   VS   (4b, 5a)
1) 30 ft./9 m. From a block, climb a wall to a cave belay.   2) 60 ft./18 m. Step R, then move L across the cave lip and finish by a fine edge.

38   Wildcat Tor

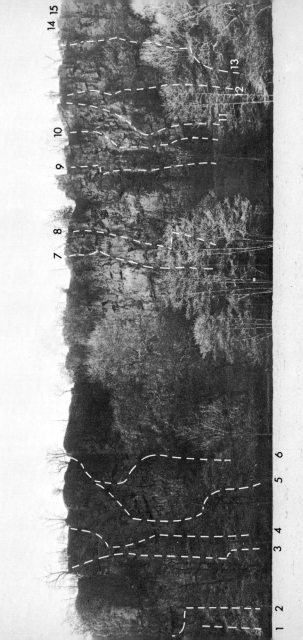

**38.13 Lynx S (4a, 4a)
1) 90 ft./27 m. Go up to a big tree. Climb a wall above, going L to ledges (tree belay). 2) 50 ft./15 m. Climb steep corners and finish up a steep crack.

***38.14 Great Cleft HVS (4a, 5b)
1) 90 ft./27 m. As 38.13. 2) 60 ft./18 m. Climb a groove with difficulty to the steep crack (PR below it). Ascend the crack using jams.

**38.15 Sphynx VS (4a, 4c)
1) 60 ft./18 m. Go up to the large tree and move up the wall. TR R to the edge and use good holds to reach a tree stance. 2) 60 ft./18 m. Move L and go straight up to the O/H. TR L, move up and climb steep cracks before exiting L.

***38.16 Cataclysm VS (4b, 5a)
1) 50 ft./15 m. Climb up a steep groove and wall to a cave (PB). 2) 60 ft./18 m. Enter a groove L of the cave and climb direct to the O/H (PR). Move R and make a hard final move.

38.17 Metamorphosis HVS (5a, 5a)
1) 35 ft./11 m. Climb wall R of cave of 38.16 to enter it. 2) 80 ft./24 m. Go R and pull over roof. Climb R by rib and finish by wall R of 38.16.

Willersley Castle Crag (OS Ref 296570)
Secludedly situated in the Cromford church grounds by the Derwent and only a few yards from the A6, this cliff provides very steep limestone climbing. It is north-facing and thus occasionally slow to dry in winter, but shelter from the wind is a compensation of winter days. The crag is approached in five minutes via iron gates near the Cromford junction.

39.1 The Grasper 50 ft./15 m. HVS (5b)
Jam the overhanging crack to the ledge (PB). Exit L.

*39.2 **The Great Corner**   50 ft./15 m.   S   (4a)
Jam the corner-crack to a ledge (PB). Exit L.

*39.2A **Zombie**
1) 70 ft./21 m. E1 (5b). Climb the steep crack just R of the
corner to a ledge.   2) 70 ft./21 m. Easier ground to the top.

*39.2B **God**
1) 70 ft./21 m. E1 (5b). Climb a steep crack over bulges to a
steep groove. Move L to the stance above.   2) 70 ft./21 m. as
above.

***39.3 **Lime Street Direct**   HVS   (5b, 4c)
1) 90 ft./27 m. TR L from the groove (39.4) to below a bulge.
Climb this and a second one to a standing place. Continue to
grassy ledges.   2) 50 ft./5 m. Take an O/H on the R and move R
to an overhanging wall below a bent tree. Direct start is 5c.

***39.4 **Lone Tree Groove**   HVS   (5a, 4c)
1) 90 ft./27 m. The crack on the L wall is followed past an O/H
to a small tree. Continue up the corner and exit by difficult
moves on the L wall (PB).   2) 40 ft./12 m. TR R and go up on
good hand-holds to the groove below the dead tree (PR). Climb
the groove past the tree.

*39.5 **Sycamore Flake**   VS   (4c, 4c)
1) 60 ft./18 m. Follow the flake beyond the tree until it merges
into the wall, mantelshelf and climb the wall into the chimney
(PB).   2) 80 ft./24 m. Climb the O/H and groove until an escape
up ledges into 39.6.

*39.6 **Babylon Groove**   HVS   (5a)
1) 75 ft./23 m. Climb a green and frequently slippery groove
past small trees to belay below an O/H (PB).   2) 60 ft./18 m.
Pull over a bulge and move up to O/H. TR L to a crack which
leads to a bay. Move R to a tree belay.   3) 20 ft./6 m. Escape
up easy ledges.

*39.6A **Last Testament**   E2   (5c)

1) 120 ft./36 m. Start in groove L of 39.7. Go R to a thin crack and up to o/H. Step L, pass the o/H (PR) and follow indefinite cracks above to blocks (PR). Finish by a gully.

39.7   **Guts Ache Groove   VS   (4c, 4b)

1) 70 ft./21 m. The groove gives excellent bridging to a stance on the R (PB).   2) 40 ft./12 m. Finish up L.

***39.8   **Garrotter**   VS   (4a, 4c)

1) 50 ft./15 m. The initial groove leads past an o/H to a move L to a large ledge.   2) 70 ft./21 m. Pass large blocks and continue up a series of fine cracks.

***39.9   **Pothole Wall**   VS   (4c, 4c)

1) 70 ft./21 m. Climb the steep corner past a bulge and steep moves to an o/H stance (PB).   2) 60 ft./18 m. Go R with difficulty past the pot-hole. Move back L above and finish up earthy ledges.

39.10   **Gangue Grooves   HVS   (5b, 5a)

1) 70 ft./21 m. Go up a steep wall and stand on a horizontal ledge. Move L and climb the very steep friable grooves (small runners) to a small stance below overhangs.   2) 70 ft./21 m. Move R and TR the slab. Climb a groove (2 PR) and step L to finish.

39.11   **Overhanging Wall   VS   (4c, 4c)

1) 60 ft./18 m. A steep wall leads to a TR L at 20 ft./6 m. The short groove is awkward. Belay on the R (PB).   2) 60 ft./18 m. Take the steep wall above to a tree and the groove above and finish on the R.

*39.12   **PTO**   HVS   (5a, 5a)

1) 45 ft./14 m. A very steep wall and groove lead to a constricted stance (PB) under the roof.   2) 55 ft./17 m. Overcome the o/H (1 PR). Finish via a flake on the L or by a groove in the direct line.

***39.13 **Boomerang** HVS (5b, 4a)
1) 80 ft./24 m. Ascend slabs by a diagonal line to the R to a PR.
Make a difficult move R and climb into the scoop (1 PR). Climb
the fingery corner by layaway and bridging moves to a
ledge.   2) 40 ft./12 m. Finish up vegetated rocks.

39.14 **Cucumber Groove   80 ft./24 m.   VS   (4b)
Follow the groove past two small trees to a small ledge and
continue direct.

39.14A **Cucumber Variant**   80 ft./24 m.   VS   (4c)
Climb the corner to tree, move R across rib and go up a groove
R to finish.

39.14B **Sisyphus**   70 ft./21 m.   E2   (5c)
Take an arête to a thin crack. Make hard move R, step L to
another thin crack and finish as 39.14A.

39.14C **Adamant**   65 ft./20 m.   VS   (5a)
From a wobbly stone, climb the crack direct.

39.14D **Constable Crack**   65 ft./20 m.   HVS   (5b)
From the stance, follow a crack R past O/H. Go L and back R via
an overhanging crack.

*39.15 **White Wall Corner**   80 ft./24 m.   VS   (4c)
Climb blocks L of the corner and move R into it. Go direct up to
the roof and exit L, with difficulty, on to a ledge. Finish up a
short rib.

Black Rocks   (OS Ref 293558)
The forbidding bouldery towers of Black Rocks dominate the
skyline one mile to the south of Cromford, in sharp contrast to
the white limestone walls of the Matlock gorge. Serious
gritstone climbing of all standards is sanctified by long-
standing usage. The Wirksworth road is taken from Cromford,
until a lane leads south towards the cliff. It can be reached in
less than half an hour's walk from the village.

40   Black Rocks South

*40.1 **Pseudonym**   50 ft./15 m.   E5   (6a)
Climb the ramp to a bulge, attain the slab and break above. Tʀ
ʟ to the gully, then move back ʀ up the arête to finish. The
break is Fun Traverse (E4, 6a).

40.1A **Lone Tree Gully**   50 ft./15 m.   VD   (3b)
From a shallow cave, take cracks which lead to a stance on the
ʟ. It is possible to finish direct or on the ʟ.

*40.2 **Lone Tree Groove**   55 ft./17 m.   VS   (4c)
Follow the groove to the o/ʜ. Overcome the crack, using arm
and knee wedges, until it eases.

40.3 **Demon Rib   60 ft./18 m.   E3   (5c)
Pull on to an overhung shelf, layback the crack above and
climb the rib with difficulty. Unprotected.

***40.4 **Birch Tree Wall**   90 ft./27 m.   VS   (5a)
Climb the thin crack on the ʟ and Tʀ ʀ at 10 ft./3 m. to the main
crack, which can also be ascended direct. Go up to the block
(belay). Tʀ ʟ along the scoop.

40.5 **Curving Arête   35 ft./11 m.   E5   (6b)
Pull on to the arête (crux) and follow it. Serious.

***40.6 **Gaia**   35 ft./11 m.   E8   (7a)
Climb the arête to the bulge and move ʀ into the hanging
scoop, and ascend it.

41.1 **Lean Man's Superdirect   60 ft./18 m.   VS   (4c)
An overhanging chimney is climbed by layback to a stance on
the buttress front (belay). A thin overhanging crack is followed
to a delicate steep finish on small holds.

41.2 **Lean Man's Climb   65 ft./20 m.   VS   (4c)
The polished crack is precariously laybacked to the stance. A
crack above is climbed to a step ʟ. The final crack is jammed.

41.3 **Sand Buttress**   70 ft./21 m.   HVS   (4c)
The overhanging crack is followed to its end. Tr L in an
exposed situation, make a hard move up to a perched block
(belay). Move up and TR R on to the arête above the gully,
which is climbed with difficulty.

41.4 **Stonnis Crack**   35 ft./11 m.   S   (4a)
Jam the crack to a steep exit. Finish up a short crack.

41.5 **Stonnis Buttress**   100 ft./30 m.   D   (2b)
Climb a crack to a shelf and move L. Follow a slab R to the
arête. Ascend it by gripping the rock with the knees, finishing
up a short wall (unprotected).

41.6 **Promontory Traverse**   80 ft./24 m.   HVS   (5b)
Start in the R-hand gully. Hand-TR to a niche (bar). Move up
and TR L delicately to a very hard step-up on to a ledge
(possible stance). Move down L with difficulty and TR to a
spike, move up and continue at a higher level.
V   It is possible to exit over the nose from the arête stance.

41.6A **Rope Trick**   65 ft./20 m.   E1   (5c)
From high in L Promontory Gully, TR lower break to ledge on
arête. Climb the o/H and niche above.

41.6B **Firebird**   45 ft./14 m.   E2   (5c)
From L gully, follow the second horizontal break R to below the
spike on the TR. Move up and R to the spike and up the crack
above.

41.7 **Blind Man's Buttress**   55 ft./17 m.   VD   (3b)
Tr L from the gully and move on to the slab. Move R and follow
the R edge on polished holds to a grass ledge. Finish up a crack.

41.8 **Central Buttress**   70 ft./21 m.   VD   (3b)
Tr the base of Stonnis Pinnacle to the R. Go up a slab to a
stance and continue up the slab centre to a ledge on the R.
Move up and L with difficulty and finish direct.

41.6A   Keith Sharples on Rope Trick, Black Rocks

41.9 **Black Crack** 30 ft./9 m. VS (4c)
Jam the crack exiting R. Easier above.

41.10 **Green Crack** 30 ft./9 m. VS (4c)
Layback or jam the crack to a hard finish.

41.11 **Pine Tree Gully** 40 ft./12 m. D (2b)
Chimney up the L side of the gully.

41.12 **Queen's Parlour Chimney** 90 ft./27 m.
VD (3b)
Up easy slabs to the chimney and back and foot this, moving on
to a ledge on the R. Go up to the terrace, exiting R.

41.13 **Original Route 90 ft./27 m. VD (2c)
Follow 41.12, but go inside the chimney to the cave. Pull out on
to the terrace and finish by a hard crack. Many variations are
possible.

41.14 **Queen's Parlour Gully** 85 ft./26 m. D (2b)
The gully is climbed by various routes to an o/H which can be
avoided on the R.

41.15 **Queen's Parlour Slab** 45 ft./14 m. (4b)
Start by a TR R from midway level in the gully. Make an
awkward mantelshelf or escape on to the terrace above (41.12).

*41.15B **Mental Pygmy** 25 ft./8 m. E3 (6a)
Start L of 41.15 and climb the wall to the roof crack. Finish over
the o/H.

Cratcliffe Tor (OS Ref 228623)
Beautifully situated, this compact gritstone outcrop faces south
and provides classic climbing of all standards. It is quickly
reached from the A524.

42.1 **Hermitage Crack** 25 ft./8 m. S (4b)
The short curved crack is jammed and left by a move R to reach
the terrace.

42   Cratcliffe Tor

125

42.1A **Reticent Mass Murderer**   25 ft./8 m.   E5   (6b)
From a terrace above 42.1, climb the overhanging crack.

42.1B **Genocide**   25 ft./8 m.   E5   (6b)
Climb a flake until it disappears R of 42.1A.

*42.2 **Giant's Staircase**   60 ft./18 m.   VS   (4a)
Move up R and ascend shelves by mantelshelf. Escape L by a
steep smooth mantelshelf on to a ledge (belay). Escape by a
pull out to the L and a TR.

42.3 **Tom Thumb   60 ft./18 m.   E2   (5c)
Climb crack above 42.4 and move L to a good ledge. Move R
across O/H and pull into finishing groove.

42.3A **Beanstalk**   50 ft./15   E2   (5c)
Climb a difficult crack and move R with difficulty on to a rib,
then follow it.

42.4 **Bramble Groove**   50 ft./15 m.   S   (3c)
From a short chimney, step L to a ledge. Climb the groove and
overhanging crack on the L.

*42.5 **Elliott's Unconquerable**   30 ft./9 m.   HVS   (5a)
Jam and layback the crack to a horizontal ledge. Exit direct, on
the R or L.

42.6 **Weston's Chimney**   50 ft./15 m.   VD   (3b)
Climb large blocks from the R. Exit up the cleft above the
blocks and to the R.

***42.7 **Boothill**   60 ft./18 m.   (5c)
Move R on to the arête and climb it with long reaches, either on
the face or by a deviation onto the L face. Boot boy (E4, 6b) is a
direct variation up the lower arête.

***42.8 **Fernhill**   50 ft./15 m.   E2   (5c)
TR the fierce diagonal line L out of 42.9 and finish R of the O/H
of Owl Buttress. There is a lower variation (E3, 5c).

42.9 **Owl Gully**   60 ft./18 m.   D   (2b)
Ascend the v-groove, exiting on the R.

42.9A **Nettle Wine**   60 ft./18 m.   E4   (6b)
Go 10 ft./3 m. along obvious R-hand TR from 42.9 and move into upper break. Climb up and L by hanging flake.

***42.10 **Five Finger Exercise**   60 ft./18 m.   E2   (5c)
Climb wall R of 42.9 to a break. Move L and up to a flake, which is followed to the top with difficulty.

42.11 **The Bower**   35 ft./11 m.   S   (3c)
From a short slab, swing R on good handholds to reach a short jamming crack. Climb it to the tree. (Abseil exit.)

***42.12 **Requiem**   90 ft./27 m.   E3   (6a)
Climb the O/H R of the 42.11 and a second bulge to join that route – B in 42.11. Enter a crack at the R end of the O/HS. TR L on jams, move up and climb very steeply to the O/H. Move R and pull up a black wall to finish.

***42.13 **Suicide Wall**   90 ft./27 m.   HVS   (5a)
Pull up over a tree into a niche. Follow the crack and exit L to 42.11. Hand-TR R, pull up on small nettle-covered holds and climb steep cracks to a niche. Layback and jam the upper flake.

*42.14 **Oak Tree Chimney and North Climb**
60 ft./18 m.   VD   (3b)
Take the narrow cleft to a terrace. Walk to the R and climb a v-corner on polished jams.

42.15 **Sepulchrave**   50 ft./15 m.   HVS   (5a)
From the terrace, follow a crack for 20 ft./6 m. and TR L to the niche of 42.13. Move R and finish up a short wide crack-chimney.

42.16 **Savage Messiah   50 ft./15 m.   E2   (5c)
Climb to the break as 42.15. Take the wall direct by the pocket to the upper chimney.

42.17 **Mordaunt – Dr Prune** 220 ft./67 m. E2 (5b, 5b, 5a, 5b)

Follow 42.15 to 42.13. TR L to another niche (Runner above). Hand-TR to the arête (B round the corner). Follow Tiger Traverse in reverse to the gully (42.9). From a belay high in the gully, TR the upper break of Owl Buttress, starting from a point 10 ft./3 m. below.

Pic Tor (OS Ref 298598)

The crag is in a hidden corner, near the River Derwent, in Hall Leys Park, Matlock. From the car-park near the Boat House pub on the A6, cross a footbridge and walk towards the town. The crag is about 150 yds./140 m. on the right. It has a large selection of short technical climbs in the modern idiom. The climbs are described from L to R.

43.1 **Big Pig** 65 ft./20 m. VS (5a)

A clean groove is climbed throughout.

*43.2 **Permission** 50 ft./15 m. E3 (6a)

Climb the steep arête using the thin flake and continue on pockets.

*43.3 **Sulphur City** 60 ft./18 m. E3 (6a)

Climb the steep pocketed wall (1 BR and one thread).

*43.4 **The Impending Gleam** 65 ft./20 m. HVS (5a)

Climb a steep little crack and swing on to the arête. Climb it to a belay/descent point.

*43.5 **Burning Spear** 65 ft./20 m. HVS (5a)

Follow the fine groove until a final move L to descent point.

43.6 **Nosferatu 75 ft./23 m. E1 (5c)

A crack leads to a block and tree. Follow the thin crack, using fine pockets and a thin R-slanting crack, to easier ground.

42.10   *Five Finger Exercise. Alan Bennett*

* *43.7* **Cistron**   75 ft./23 m.   HVS   (5a)
Follow a crack to a tree, pass it and climb more or less direct up a final steep section.

** *43.8* **Silenus**   70 ft./21 m.   E2   (5b)
The white slab is taken direct to a thin crack. Finish up 43.7 (2 threads).

** *43.9* **Erasmus**   80 ft./24 m.   E2   (5c)
An o/h leads into a steep groove. Climb it to o/h, move L and finish at a yew.

** *43.10* **Diagnosis**   75 ft./23 m.   E4   (6a)
Go up the wall 6 ft./2 m. R of 43.9 to a thread R. After a hard move, continue past another thread runner and a ledge. Descend or go R to a bolt R.

*** *43.11* **Prognosis**   75 ft./23 m.   E3   (5c)
Follow a thin crack into a scoop (thread). Move R (PR) and over a bulge. Take the thin flake to a bolt belay.

* **V Prognosis**   E3 (6a)
From the PR, go L up to a thread. Go up and R past another thread to finish as 43.11.

Upper Tor   (OS Ref 295573)
The crag faces west, and is an extension southwards of Wildcat Tor. It is close to Willersley Castle, and in private grounds. It is possible to approach it from Wildcat Crag, along the riverside path and by a climb up zigzags to below the crag, or from above. It is best to avoid the castle, as approach that way causes offence. The crag gives four very good climbs, all strenuous at their standard.

* *43.12* **Liberty Cap**   70 ft./21 m.   E2   (5c)
Climb the L-hand crack, finishing up the thin crack.

43   Gary Gibson on Neurosis, Pic Tor

*****43**.13   **Great Crack**   70 ft./21 m.   E2   (5c)

Take the central crack direct, with a hard move over a bulge and wider crack above.

****43**.14   **Sunset Crack**   70 ft./21 m.   E1   (5b)

The crack on the R is attained with difficulty, and is strenuous above.

***43**.15   **Go-go Grooves**   75 ft./23 m.   HVS   (5a)

An overhanging crack is climbed to a ledge on the R. Step L and climb a steep groove and wall.

Central Derbyshire Limestone

The heartland dome of central Derbyshire is composed of mountain limestone and it is in this area that the most dramatic climbing developments in recent years have occurred. The river valleys cut gorges through the limestone, providing long cliff series with multitudes of climbing possibilities. The character of the climbing is intensely varied, both in situation and in the character of the rock itself. From the brittle, relatively small buttresses of the Winnats in the north, to the smooth white walls of Chee Dale, the brittle, black-banded rocks of Water-cum-Jolly or the semi-quarried, dusty precipice of Stoney Middleton, one proceeds in the south to the isolated pinnacles of Dovedale and the splendid solid faces of Manifold Valley. It is an area of contrasts, sheltered from the worst of the weather and giving magnificent climbing throughout the year, abutting to the north-east and west on to the bleaker hills of gritstone, and merging gently in the south into the Midland Plain.

Limestone, once thought fit only for rock-engineering using multitudes of pitons, has come of age. Artificial climbs are in a minority and the best standards of practice are as strictly prescribed as on gritstone. Care is needed in dealing wih a wide variety of serious situations caused by the looseness and angle of the rock, the greater size of the cliffs than is usual on gritstone, and the generally high technical standard. But none of these factors is now thought to justify the indiscriminate use of aid. This is regarded with as little favour upon limestone as it has traditionally been on gritstone.

Overall, it is desirable to approach limestone-climbing at least as seriously as one would a climb at Tremadoc, in Llanberis or on Gimmer Crag. Indeed, on harder modern climbs in this area, the climber's attitude and equipment need to be better prepared than is necessary for many of the hardest volcanic climbs.

Limestone is found everywhere between Castleton in the north and Ashbourne in the south, a distance of about 25 miles. It is therefore expedient to describe approaches etc., under the headings of particular sections.

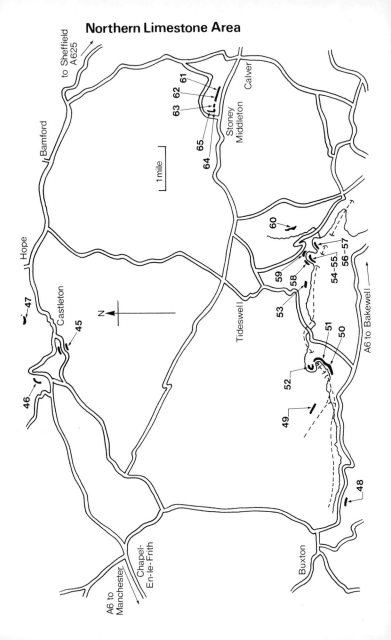

Northern Limestone Area

Castleton – Winnats Pass   (OS Ref 138827)

This unique little pass is less interesting than it appears as a
climbing ground, though it has some unique features. It is
easily reached from the village.

45.1 **Elbow Ridge**   200 ft./61 m.   D   (2a)
Climb the ridge to an easing and continue up an upper nose.
Interesting under snow.

*45.2 **Matterhorn Ridge**   200 ft./61 m.   VD   (3a)
Climb the ridge L of a hole for 40 ft./12 m., TR R and continue
direct to a grassy col. Above, there are steeper rocks to a
platform and poised block, avoided on its L. Interesting in
snow.

Shining Tor

45.3A **Rite of Way**   90 ft./27 m.   E5   (6b)
Free climb the wall, using the 20 bolts for protection.

45.3B **Do Up Your Flies**   90 ft./27 m.   E5   (6a)
Free climb the wall 30 ft./9 m. R of the cave with old PRs.

45.3C **Kaiser Bill**   80 ft./24 m.   HVS   (5a)
From L of the cave, go up 25 ft./8 m. and TR R to a crack. Climb
this past the cave, finishing on the R.

The Shield

45.4 **Gingerman**   75 ft./23 m.   HVS   (5a)
Climb the wall and groove to the O/H, (PR on L) layback it and
move R to a ledge (PR). The wall leads to a hole (PR inside) and
difficult moves lead up a groove to the top.

45.5 **Pint of Blood**   70 ft./21 m.   HVS   (5b)
Flaky blocks and loose rock lead to a P. TR L and then go up to
a groove. Climb it and finish up a crack on the R.

Castleton – Mam Tor   (OS Ref 139835)

A shale-built slag-heap of inverately crumbling rubble. Mam Tor is excellent in frozen conditions with light snow. Crampons and ice hammers are usual and midnight ascent is preferable for competent parties. All climbs are poorly protected and inadvisable in unfrozen conditions.

46.1 **The Gully**   250 ft./76 m.   M   (1c)

Ascend direct until the final steepening, which is avoided on the L. It has been descended on skis at least twice in unusually snowy conditions – a serious proposition.

46.2 **Blue John Rib**   250 ft./76 m.   VD   (3b)

Follow the R skyline of the gully. Difficult to start and to finish.

46.3 **Central Route**   250 ft./76 m.   S   (4a)

Take the centre of the L-hand scoop. The wall in the centre is the main problem (1 PR).

46.4 **Hari Kari Route**   250 ft./76 m.   S   (4a)

The R-hand scoop.

Castleton – Back Tor   (OS Ref 148852)

Similar in structure to Mam Tor, the face is northerly in aspect and remains frozen longer.

47.1 **The Gully**   200 ft./61 m.   VD   (3c)

The central scoop is the crux.

47.2 **The Face**   200 ft./61 m.   VD   (3c)

Wander the face to the R.

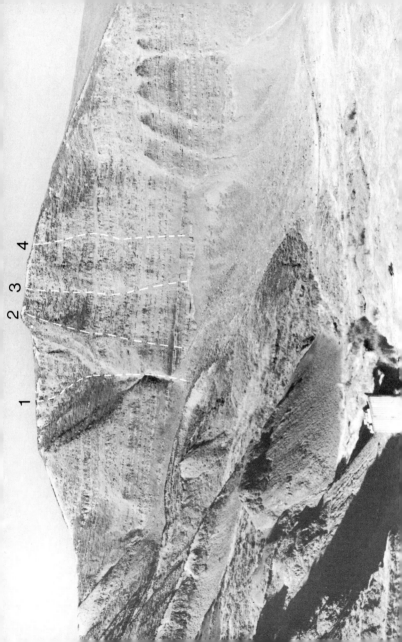

The Wye Valley

Between Buxton and Bakewell there is an immense
concentration of limestone cliffs in the Wye Gorge and its
tributary valleys.

Staidon Quarry (OS Ref 082722)

The crag is easily reached from the A6, 1½ miles east of
Buxton. It is quite extensive, with a steep central wall.
Permission to climb should be asked for at Staidon Farm.

*48.1 **Suscipiat** 100 ft./30 m. VS (4b)

A short crack leads to a ledge. The face is climbed near the
arête to a yellow niche and ledges.

48.2 **The Nails 100 ft./30 m. HVS (5a)

Up a thin crack to a break. Move into a scoop and climb a thin
crack above into a corner. Move L and back R and up the
corner.

***48.3 **Welcome to Hard Times** 100 ft./30 m.
E1 (5b)

Climb the wall to a bulge (thread) and over it, then TR a break
L to the finish off 48.2.

48.4 **Joint Effort 100 ft./30 m. HVS (5a)

Climb a thin crack, with difficulty low down.

48.5 **Captain Reliable 80 ft./24 m. E2 (5c)

At the next crack R. Climb the crack to a bulge, pass it on the L
then on the R. Finish straight up by a scarred wall.

48.6 **Cathy's Clown 80 ft./24 m. E3 (5c)

20 ft./6 m. R of 48.5. Climb a thin crack and up a wall to a
bulge. Finish direct or slightly R.

***48.7 **Liquid Courage** 80 ft./24 m. E2 (5c)

10 ft./3 m. R of 48.6. Climb cracks and calcite holds to a hard
pull over a bulge (thread). Finish slightly R.

48 Staidon Quarry

Great Rocks Dale Quarry   (OS Ref 112730)

This large quarry is visible from the A6 near Topley Pike. It is best approached by a small riverside track leaving that road at the bottom of the hill. From the railway cottages, old paths lead up to the quarry. It is very loose, in places to a dangerous extent. It is little visited as climbing is forbidden.

**49.1 'M'   HVS   (3b, 5a, 5a)

1) 30 ft./9 m. From the mound, ascend to a ledge (PB).
2) 55 ft./17 m. Climb the cracks to an overlap. Overcome it (P and sling for aid) and reach a small ledge (PB).   3) 55 ft./17 m. TR R and go up to a groove. Continue direct.

49.2 Nandin   VS   (4a, 4c, 4c)

1) 40 ft./12 m. Climb the groove R of the arête to a ledge (PB).   2) 40 ft./12 m. Move L and climb steeply R of the arête on small holds to a small stance (PB).   3) 40 ft./12 m. Move R up cracks to finish.

49.3 The Temple of Lara Jangrong   HVS   (4c, 5a, 5a)

1) 60 ft./18 m. Move up the overhanging wall, TR R to the edge and step up and L to a ledge under O/HS (PB).   2) 50 ft./15 m. Move R and climb a shallow groove on small holds. TR L to belay in an exposed position round the arête to the L (PB).   3) 65 ft./20 m. Climb the groove with a sling for aid on a protruding flake below the roof (loose).

49.4 Vishnu   HVS   (5a, 5a, 4a)

1) 50 ft./15 m. Take a L-slanting crack to the first O/H, climb it and place a PR. Go up past a bulge to a steep crack leading to a belay (P).   2) 50 ft./15 m. Go up above the belay to a flake and use 2 PA to reach a thread on the R. Use this and climb a crack to a belay.   3) 20 ft./6 m. Up a final corner.

49.5 Sanctuary of Siva   HVS   (4c, 5a, 5a)

1) 50 ft./15 m. From a tree, move up a little and TR out R to a stance (PB).   2) 35 ft./11 m. Continue traversing R (3 PA) to a stance in a groove (PB).   3) 50 ft./15 m. Climb the steep groove.

Chee Dale – Plum Buttress   (OS Ref 115726)

One of the biggest and finest features of Derbyshire rock architecture, with a few climbs to match, the buttress is easily reached in five minutes from the railway cottages. It is composed of steep, natural and generally solid limestone.

***50.1 **Sirplum**   E1   (4c, 5b)
1) 80 ft./24 m. Climb a short wall and easier angled scoop to a tree ledge on the R. A difficult scoop leads to rake (belay).   2) 100 ft./30 m. Pull over the O/H (PR) and move L to a ledge. Pull up a steep wall to a thread on the L. Climb a groove, step L and finish up a second easier groove (PR in first groove). Strenuous and overhanging climbing as spectacular as any in Derbyshire.

50.2 **The Spider   S   (4a, A3)
1) 60 ft./18 m. Ascend the groove to a ledge on the L (PB).   2) 120 ft./36 m. Move up to the roof and into its second level. TR R and over the roof (loose bolts) to a horizontal break. Up the wall above, with difficult moves on the black wall avoiding an escape into 50.1.

50.3 **Big Plum   E4   (4a, 6b, 4c)
1) 60 ft./18 m. Ascend the groove to a ledge on the L (PB).   2) 60 ft./18 m. Climb up to the roof and TR L to make strenuous moves round the lip.   3) 60 ft./18 m. Climb the cracks direct. It is also possible and easier to exit L (4a).   4) 50 ft./15 m. Follow loose cracks on the arête to the summit.

50.4 **Victoria   E2   (5a, 5c)
1) 70 ft./21 m. Trend diagonally L up the wall to a v-groove. Follow it to a bulge and the rake (1 PR).   2) 80 ft./24 m. Move over the first O/H and bridge out over the second (4 PR). Continue by easier climbing a groove.

50.5 **Stalk   90 ft./27 m.   VS   (4c)
Climb the lower wall from R to L into the corner crack. Follow the corner on good jams, exiting L at the rake.

50A   Plum Buttress, Chee Dale

***50.6 **Sarin-Aplomb** HVS (4c, 5a, 4c, 5b, 5a)
1) 55 ft./17 m. Climb on to a small ledge at 10 ft./3 m., move R
for 15 ft./4 m. and climb up to a scoop on the R. Step L then TR R
to a ledge and tree belay (PB). 2) 60 ft./18 m. TR the ledge to
its end and hand-TR to 50.5. Ascend to ledge and thread
belays. 3) 40 ft./12 m. Follow the crack of 50.5 to the ledges
on the L. 4) 50 ft./15 m. Climb a grassy wall for a few feet to
ledges and go R to a spike. TR R to belay in Big Plum Groove
(PB). 5) 90 ft./27 m. Move down and hand-TR the void above
the roofs to 50.2. Continue in similar vein to 50.1. Move R to a
small ledge (PB). 6) 60 ft./18 m. Either climb diagonally R or
ascend the groove above the stance direct, or do 50.1 to finish
(E1).

*50.7A **Ragged Arête** 70 ft./21 m. VD (3b)
Start at R end of crag L of a grassy gully. Climb the groove, then
the arête, finishing direct.

50.7 **Tendril** 80 ft./24 m. S (4a)
Follow the L-hand crack of the pinnacle on good jams, belaying
on a platform below the top.

*50.8 **Chagrin** 85 ft./26 m. HVS (5a)
A steep wall leads to a flake at 50 ft./15 m. Pull over a bulge and
climb the steep wall.

*50.9 **Cohesion Cracks** 85 ft./26 m. VS (4b)
Climb the steep groove and a crack on its L wall to a ledge.
Continue up a fine crack on the R.

*50.9A **Tika** 55 ft./17 m. S (4a)
Start 20 ft./6 m. L of 50.9 on L side of a tower; climb a groove
then R across the tower and round to a corner. Up this to a
stance. 2) 30 ft./9 m. Follow the obvious crack to finish.

50.10 **Succulent Corner 70 ft./21 m. HVS (5b)
A loose wall is climbed to the ledge below the corner crack.
Continue up this.

50B   *Chee Dale*

*50.11 **Black Edge**   60 ft./18 m.   HVS   (5b)
Climb the nose, to enter the corner. Escape L from the top of the corner.

*50.12 **Firefly Crack**   65 ft./20 m.   VS   (4c)
Ascend the fine crack direct.

50.13 **Heathenism   30 ft./9 m.   VD   (3b)
Climb the short side of the Obelisk. Abseil descent.

50.14 **Vibration**   HVS   (5a, 4a)
1) 80 ft./24 m. Climb the slanting rake leading R to a ledge (1 PR). Climb cracks to an O/H, swing L and reach a terrace.   2) 20 ft./6 m. Climb a corner crack.

V Quake   HVS   (5b)
Climb a crack 30 ft./9 m. R of 50.14 to a thread. Move TR to a groove and climb it to the ledge of 50.14.

*50.14A **Calvi Corner**   100 ft./30 m.   S   (4a)
The obvious large corner.

*50.15 **Thin Thin Groove**   VS   (4c, 4a)
1) 90 ft./27 m. A narrow rib leads to the O/H. Pull into the groove and climb with difficulty to a step R. Continue with difficulty to a terrace.   2) 15 ft./4 m. Continue up the wall.

50.16 **Dangleberry   VS   (4b, 4c)
1) 45 ft./14 m. Climb to the niche under O/Hs, swing R and mantelshelf on to a narrow ledge (PB).   2) 55 ft./17 m. Climb the crack awkwardly and exit R to the terrace.   3) 30 ft./9 m. Move R and climb a steep wall, using a tree.

50.17 **Oscillation**   VS   (4b, 3c)
1) 85 ft./26 m. Climb the corner to a horizontal crack, which allows an exit TR on to the arête. Up a groove to the terrace.   2) 35 ft./11 m. Up the obvious chimney. The lower groove direct is harder (5a).

50.1   Sirplum Chee Dale, Bob Dearman leading

148

50.17A **Thin Lizzy** 70 ft./21 m. HVS (5a)
Start at a curving groove and climb to a break. Move TR and climb the o/H and finish up a further groove.

50.18 **Monoton** 100 ft./30 m. VS (4c)
A steep groove leads to the break. Move R to ledge. An awkward groove is taken to the terrace.

50.19 **Whistling Crack** 100 ft./30 m. S (4a)
Follow the steep black crack throughout, avoiding occasional loose blocks.

50.20 **Moving Buttress Traverse** E1 (4c, 5a, 5c, 4c, 5c)
1) 45 ft./14 m. From 50.14A TR L under o/Hs and mantelshelf on to a ledge (PR). Move L to a PB in a recess. 2) 80 ft./24 m. Follow a ledge to an awkward move (PR beyond it). Pass a dead tree, move down and cross a groove to a ledge (PB). 3) 80 ft./24 m. Move down and TR under o/H. Move L (PR) to belay. 4) 90 ft./27 m. Follow ledges and cross a final steep section (thread runners) to 50.19. 5) 85 ft./26 m. Go out to the arête and follow the crack into a corner (thread runners). Climb it to the terrace.

Chee Dale Two-Tier Buttress (OS Ref 123728)

51.1A **Machineries of Joy** HVS (5a, 5b)
1) 90 ft./27 m. (5b) Start just L of the descent gully on the R of the crag. Climb a flaky wall and crack to the o/H (PR). Move R and belay in gully. 2) 30 ft./9 m. (5a) Climb the wall above the gully.

51.1B **Mad Dogs and Englishmen** 100 ft./30 m. E3 (5c)
Climb as for 51.1A to the PR. Step L to a flake and climb it to the o/H. Move L and over the o/H. TR R to a final groove.

***51.1 **Chicken Run** HVS (5a, 5a)
1) 80 ft./24 m. Climb the corner (PR) to a ledge. 2) 45 ft./
14 m. Move R and climb the steep black, flake crack to finish; or
escape more easily R below.

***51.2 **Darl** E5 (6a, 6b)
1) 80 ft./24 m. From a trampled landing, climb the bulging
wall past a sapling and up a groove. Move L and up to
jungle. 2) 40 ft./12 m. Climb the steep crack and wall above.

51.3 **Stolen Fruit 80 ft./24 m. E2 (6a)
Climb the L wall of the large corner for 20 ft./6 m. TR R to a
break and enter a thin crack. Up this moving R to an easing of
angle, then finish direct.

51.4 **Malnutrition 100 ft./30 m. E3 (5c)
At the next corner L, climb the groove and move R to a ledge.
Go up over the O/H and up L to a ledge. Finish direct.

51.5 **Thoth HVS (5b, 5a)
1) 45 ft./14 m. Climb the groove to a break. TR R to a
tree. 2) 65 ft./20 m. Move L and climb the groove past the O/H
beyond which it eases.

The Nook
300 yds./270 m. downriver, on the opposite
bank to Two Tier Buttress.

51.6 **Santiano E3 (6a)
Start below big O/H. Climb up and over the roof, using cunning
legwork in the niche. Finish direct.

Chee Tor (OS Ref 124733)
Together with Plum Buttress, this cliff is the finest in the Wye
valley. It is reached, via the railway, in 20 minutes from the
railway cottages, from Millers Dale or from Wormhill.

52.1 **Gulle Gulle Groove** HVS (4c, 5b)

1) A R-slanting groove is climbed for 50 ft./15 m. where the crack ends. Move R (PR) and climb further cracks to the rake. 2) 40 ft./12 m. Move L to a hanging groove and enter it with difficulty. Easier, but dirty, climbing follows.

52.2 **The Chopper** HVS (5a)

1) 90 ft./27 m. Climb the wall L of the groove to a PR. Trend gently L up the wall on flaky cracks to ledges below the rake, and go L to a large stance by a tree. 2) 60 ft./18 m. Up the chimney.

52.3 **42nd Street** 130 ft./40 m. E2 (5c)

A shallow groove ends at 20 ft./16 m. Hand-TR L to a sapling and thin crack which leads on to a steep wall. Climb it on small holds, starting a little to the R and trending L to the rake. Go R to the trees. (Escape by 50.2.)

52.4 **Queer Street** 85 ft./26 m. E3 (6a)

Climb a very steep shallow groove, making difficult moves to reach a steep slab. Go up it L to a thin flake, up this and L on better holds to the rake. Yew belay. (Escape by 50.3 or abseil).

52.4A **Autobahn – Body Line** E5 (6b, 5c)

1) 80 ft./24 m. Climb a steep flake. When it finishes, go L, then direct to the yews. 2) 65 ft./20 m. From the yew, follow the old aid route to finish (free!).

52.5 **Shake** 80 ft./24 m. HVS (5b)

Climb diagonally R to join a flake and follow it to better ledges on the R. Straight up to belay on a thread at the rake. (As above.)

52.6 **Great Central Route** E1 (5a, 5c)

1) 100 ft./30 m. Climb the steep shallow groove (1 PR) and exit R to a tree. Move out R (PR) to a crack. Either climb it to the rake and move R to belay, or TR R with a high PR to a ledge (PB). 2) 70 ft./21 m. Move L and enter the groove. Climb it to the O/H and PR. Continue direct or exit R, finishing up a short groove.

**52.7 Ceramic   80 ft./24 m.   E6   (6a)

Start L of 52.6, below a clean shallow groove. Climb up the wall and groove direct to the rake. From threads, go up 10 ft./3 m. and TR R to a PR. Finish via a flake and corner.

*52.8 Valentine   HVS   (5a, 4c)

1) 80 ft./24 m. Climb a steep wall into a scooped area at 35 ft./11 m. Trend L into a groove leading to the rake (PB).   2) 65 ft./20 m. Move R and use 2 bolts and a sling to reach less steep rock. Climb a long flake to a short groove finish. Free E3 (6b).

52.9 Meditation   100 ft./30 m.   E1   (5b)

Start L of 52.8 below a groove. Climb this, then go R to join 52.6. Up an R to a scoop. Climb this to the girdle.

***52.9A Golden Mile   E5   (6b)

1) 85 ft./26 m. Climb a white groove R of 52.10. Move R to a sapling and up to ledge. Move L and climb the wall above, finishing via a little groove to the break.

***52.10 Mortlock's Arête   E4   (6a, 5c)   E4   (6a, 5c)

1) 85 ft./26 m. (6a). 25 ft./8 m. L of 52.8 is an obvious arête. Climb the crack to the arête and up this to a ledge.
2) 50 ft./15 m. (5c). Climb the shallow groove on the R.

***52.10A Tequila Mockingbird   E7   (6c)

1) 85 ft./26 m. Climb the smooth wall L of 52.10. 2 bolt and 2 PRS.

***52.10B Boo   E6   (6c)

1) 85 ft./26 m. Takes the next wall left. 3 BR.

52.11 Hurgiani   E2   (5c, 4c)

1) 95 ft./29 m. A steep wall is climbed to a flake (PR). Move R and climb the wall to a small tree and steep shallow groove below the terrace.   2) 55 ft./17 m. A short groove on the R is climbed. TR R and climb a groove of trees.

52.12 **Oblomov**   E2   (5c, 4c)

1) 50 ft./15 m. A steep wall is climbed past tiny saplings. A crack ends above. Move L (thread) and climb a slab to a tree.   2) 35 ft./11 m. Climb the ramp and swing back R to finish (PR).

***52.13 **Chee Tor Girdle Traverse**   VS   (4b, 4b, 4b, 4c, 4c)

One of the best of its genus in Derbyshire.   1) 100 ft./30 m. Climb the crack to the terrace. Thread belay on L.
2) 140 ft./43 m. TR L, with a long step down near the end, to the tree terrace of 52.20.   3) 100 ft./30 m. TR the rake, with magnificent threads to belay at the yew.   4) 120 ft./36 m. Continue more awkwardly to the arête, and strenuously with ½ PR to a small stance (PB).   5) 80 ft./24 m. TR L into the corner (2 PR) and move L to easier ground. Tree belay. Either abseil off or exit through brambles with discomfort.

52.14 **Tropic of Cancer**   HVS   (5a, 5a, 5b, 5a, 5a)

An upper-level TR from L to R. Start from the terrace of 52.11.   1) 80 ft./24 m. Climb the crack (pitch 2 of 52.11) to a horizontal crack, TR R 30 ft./9 m. to a PR and on to a small tree (PB).   2) 90 ft./27 m. Follow the line to a PR in the corner. Move R to a groove and round the arête to a thread. Cross the wall (3 PA) to a corner. Up this a few feet to a large tree.
3) 80 ft./24 m. From R edge of ledge, descend R past large flakes to a sapling. Continue to a tree belay.   4) 90 ft./27 m. Descend and use 1 PA to reach 52.6, cross it and continue to a small tree. Hand-TR to a tree belay.   5) 50 ft./15 m. Hand-TR to a tree belay in the gully (1 PR). Scramble off.

Raven Tor   (OS Ref 153733)

A black-streaked overhanging cliff overlooking the road from the Angler's Rest (Millers Dale) to Litton Mill, it yields some of Derbyshire's most interesting climbing.

53.1 Koran E4 (6b)

1) 110 ft./33 m. A short steep wall leads to a bulge. Pull on to an upper scoop (PR). TR R to a loose crack and ascend to the rake (2 loose PR). Move L (1 PR). Move L (1 PR). Go up the wall, slightly R, to stance (PB). 2) 30 ft./9 m. Up steep loose rock to finish. Serious.

53.2 Hubris E5 (6b)

1) 120 ft./36 m. Follow the old aid route with protection mainly in place.

53.3 Indecent Exposure E6 (6b, 6b)

1) 100 ft./30 m. Climb a wall and overlap R, with protection in place, to the bedding. Ascend a bulge and slight groove and TR R to 53.4 stance. 2) 65 ft./20 m. TR R round arête and follow a faint line to top. Bolt and peg protection throughout.

53.4 Prow E7 (6b, 6b, 6c)

1) 70 ft./21 m. As for 53.3 to first break, TR R and follow bolt line to break. TR to belay on R. 2) 35 ft./11 m. Move L and up to good holds, then up L to stance. 3) 55 ft./17 m. Climb direct over the Prow to finish.

*** **V Direct Start – Revelations** E7 (6c)

Climb direct to join Prow. Bolt RS.

53.5 Rooster Booster E6 (6c, 6b)

1) 50 ft./15 m. Start as 53.6. TR L above roof (PRS). Belay or pull ropes through and continue. 2) 95 ft./29 m. Climb black wall direct and L (bolt RS) until holds lead R to girdle and finish up wall above.

53.6 Sardine E5 (6b)

1) 100 ft./30 m. (6b). Start up, then L and back R to enter the crack proper (bolt). Climb the wall, passing a further bolt to break and finish direct. Very strenuous.

53.7 Cream Team Special E5 (6a, 6b)

The obvious TR line. The grades are from L to R, which is slightly easier to lead and less serious for the second than R to L.

Water-cum-Jolly   (OS Ref 160730-173737)

This enclosed valley of river and limestone cliffs is very
sheltered, but the river has been rather spoilt by damming at
Cressbrook and other minor works. It is best approached via
Millers Dale and Litton Mill to the west, or from Cressbrook to
the east. A good path runs down the north side of the river, but
access is more awkward for the south bank (see plan). All
climbs can be reached in about half an hour from Litton Mill or
Cressbrook Mill.

Climbs are found on the north and south banks. The rock is
variable and steep limestone.

Water-cum-Jolly – Central Buttress   (OS Ref 164730)

**54.1 Knuckleknocker   E2   (5c, 5a)

1) 40 ft./12 m. A wall is climbed and the o/H passed to a stance
(PB).   2) 90 ft./27 m. An obvious steep crack is climbed to a
good ledge. Pass an o/H on the R and go up to a ledge. Move R
and up to a tree. Belay well back.

**54.1A Alien   E4   (6a)

1) 110 ft./33 m. (5c). Start R of 54.2. Climb the steep wall to the
scoop. Move R to a break (P), then up L to a crack. Move R (P)
and climb steeply L to a ledge. Up R to a large ledge.

**54.2 Crumbling Cracks   VS   (4c, 4b)

1) 40 ft./12 m. A disintegrated wall leads to a good ledge on the
L.   2) 60 ft./18 m. A wide chimney crack is climbed
direct.   3) 30 ft./9 m. An easy ascent of the upper chimney.

**54.3 Troll   E1   (5c, 5a)

1) 50 ft./15 m. Climb a black splintery wall to the o/H. Move R
(PR). Belay as 54.2.   2) 70 ft./21 m. Ascend to the o/H in the
chimney. Move L to a shallow groove and follow it and a crack
above to the large ledge.   3) 30 ft./9 m. An easy ascent of the
upper chimney.

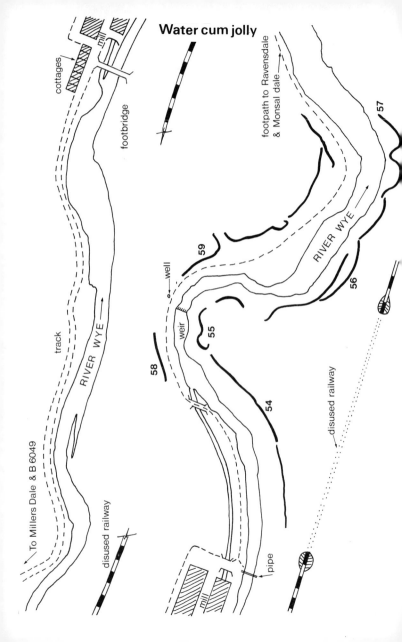

Water cum jolly

To Millers Dale & B 6049

cottages

mill

footbridge

track

RIVER WYE

disused railway

well

weir

59

58

55

54

56

57

footpath to Ravensdale & Monsal dale

RIVER WYE

disused railway

pipe

mill

***54.4 **Behemoth** E5 (5b, 6b)
1) 35 ft./11 m. Climb to the o/h and move L and up to a stance on the L (loose). PB. 2) 85 ft./26 m. Ascend L and up to a fingery crack and continue to the tree belay.

54.5 **St Paul E1 (5b)
1) 35 ft./11 m. Climb a groove (1 PR) to a ledge (PB). 2) 85 ft./26 m. Ascend the bulging wall (PR), and a groove and detached pinnacle to finish.

54.6 **The Creeper** E3 (4c, 5b, 5c, 4a, 4c, 5c, 4b)
1) 100 ft./30 m. From the little cave TR R with difficulty (PR), to reach 54.5. 2) 110 ft./33 m. Move R`(PR) on to the black buttress. Continue R to the ledge of 54.2. 3) 60 ft./18 m. From the R end of the ledge, move R to reach easier climbing. TR to a belay (PB). 4) 30 ft./9 m. Move round and down to a belay. 5) 60 ft./18 m. Steep grass and rock are crossed to steep white rock (PR). TR R to a belay. 6) 100 ft./30 m. Move down to small ledges. Reach a niche and ledges. 7) 30 ft./9 m. TR R to a crack and descend a jamming-crack to the ground.

Water-cum-Jolly – Church Buttress (OS Ref 165731)
The isolated buttress is about 50 yds./46 m. east of Central Buttress and near the way down. It is composed of good white limestone.

55.1 **Ribcrusher Crack** 45 ft./14 m. VS (4c)
Enter a sentry box and exit past a tree and final crack.

*55.1A **Ringmaster** 50 ft./15 m. E1 (5b)
Start L of 55.1 below a flake crack. Up the wall and bulge to enter the crack. Climb the crack finishing R.

55.2 **Sermon Wall** 65 ft./20 m. VS (4c)
Climb the crack to the o/h, move L and enter a steep groove (1 PA), climbing it with difficulty. An exit R is possible.

*55.3 **Vicar's Vertigo** 65 ft./20 m. E1 (5b)
The initial wall is climbed awkwardly to the groove. Climb the roof and final wall.

Water-cum-Jolly – The Cornice   (OS Ref 166729)

An excellent overhang with concentrated technical artificial climbing, without excessive length and suitable for short visits. A long peg is desirable to belay on the grass bank above.

56.1 **Convulsion**   70 ft./21 m.   A3

After 2 bolts, peg the roof with difficulty and very long reaches (2 bolts, 20 pegs).

56.2* **Nemesis   70 ft./21 m.   A3

Use 3 bolts to reach the roof. Peg the roof to a grassy finish (3 bolts, 15–20 pegs).

56.3 **Fail Safe**   70 ft./21 m.   A2

Straightforward climbing up the wall (1 bolt). There is also a lip-TR (250 ft./76 m., A3).

Water-cum-Jolly – Moat Buttress   (OS Ref 169727)

The black and ferocious-looking loose walls overhang the sinister lake above Cressbrook Mill.

57.1 **Moat Wall**   A2   VS   (4c)

1) 60 ft./18 m. Free climb to a scoop, use aid to exit from this and free-climb the groove (3 pegs, 2 bolts).   2) 50 ft./15 m. A crack and overhanging groove without pegs!

57.2 **Triton**   E2   (5c, 4c)

1) 90 ft./27 m. (5c). Start just R of the lake. Climb the wall L to a ledge. Move up the wall to a ledge, TR R to a groove and up this to belay on the R.   2) 30 ft./9 m. (4c). As for 57.1.

57.3 **Piranha Wall**   E2   (5c)

1) 100 ft./30 m. (5c). Start as for 57.1 (1) then TR diagonally L to a ledge. Finish L (PB).   2) 50 ft./15 m. Peg the flake on the L and TR pockets to a tree.

Water-cum-Jolly – The Upper Circle
Jackdaw Point   OS Ref 164733

On the L bank, 130 yds./118 m. from Litton Mill, is:

58.1A **The Vision**   60 ft./18 m.   E3   (6b)
Climb a steep wall up the face and a crack above (bolt and PR).

*58.1 **Fledgling Flakes**   HVS   (5b, 5c)
1) 60 ft./18 m. Climb a loose wall and use 1 PA to step L to more
flakes. Belay on the central ledge (PB).   2) 20 ft./6 m. Climb
the steep wall (1 PR).

58.2 **Fledgling**   70 ft./21 m.   VS   (4c)
Climb the slanting crack to the ledge (PB). Ascend the upper
wall (1 PR) as 58.1.

58.3 **Bang and Dangle**   60 ft./18 ft.   A1
Climb an obvious line of bolts. Peg the roof to L or R (5 bolts, 10
pegs).

*58.4 **Dead Tree Groove**   60 ft./18 m.   VS   (4c)
TR a slab into the groove and climb it direct (1 PR).

58.5 **Dead Tree Crack**   40 ft./12 m.   S   (4a)
Climb the crack (1 PR).

58.6 **Christmas Cracks**   50 ft./15 m.   VS   (4c)
Move up to the flakes with difficulty and climb them (loose)
with some difficulty. Move L, climb the corner and exit R to a
ledge and short wall.

59.1 **Matto Grosso Chimney**   40 ft./12 m.   VS   (4c)
Climb the wall 10 ft./3 m. R of the chimney to a ledge
(PB).   2) 50 ft./15 m. TR L (hard) to the chimney, climb it and
exit on to grass (loose).

*59.2 **Marsh Dweller's Rib**   85 ft./26 m.   E1   (5c)
Use a tree to pass an O/H and free-climb the upper section.

57   *Moat Buttress, Water-cum-Jolly*

**59.3 Ping 80 ft./24 m. HVS (5a)
Climb the L arête and move R to a crack (PR). Climb the crack to a ledge and finish up a wider crack.

*59.4 Pong HVS (5b)
Pull over an initial bulge and enter a groove on the R with difficulty. It is climbed on loose holds.

*59.5 Virgin's Crack 50 ft./15 m. S (3c)
Climb the fine wide crack.

**59.6 Bowstring Groove VS (3a, 4c)
30 ft./9 m. Easy rocks lead to a cave.   2) 40 ft./12 m. Swing over the O/H and climb the crack-groove.

*59.7 The Keep 60 ft./18 m. VD (3a)
A chimney on the L leads to the chimney. Either climb it (4a) or move R and climb the tower to its summit. Jump alarmingly off on to the hillside.

Rubicon Wall

**59.8 Dragonflight 55 ft./17 m. E2 (5c)
Start below a prominent flake and climb it to a scooped slab. Climb this to a break, move L and surmount the O/H to a grassy finish.

*59.9 Jezebel 50 ft./15 m. E5 (6b)
Climb to BR. Go up and R to finish up a flake.

**59.10 Jaws 60 ft./18 m. E5 (6b)
Climb to PR 16 ft./5 m. R of 59.9. Go up wall to ledges. Finish up wall above.

**59.11 Piranha 65 ft./20 m. E5 (6b)
From shot holes, climb wall to breaks and up bulging wall above L.

58.1A   Chris Gore climbing The Vision, Water-cum-Jolly

***59.12 **Whitebait**   65 ft./20 m.   E5   (6c)
6 ft./2 m. R of above. Pass a bulge to the pocket and go direct up the wall above (PRS) to break. Finish up wall and o/H on L.

***59.13 **Rubicon**   60 ft./18 m.   E3   (5c)
From below the large o/H, climb the wall to the roof and cross it (PRS) to an easy finish. From the lip, No Jug No Thug goes out L to a flake and ledge, finishing by a bulge above (E5, 6a).

*59.14 **Toenail Pie**   40 ft./12 m.   HVS   (5a)
Climb the overhanging wall on the R to a thread, move R and into a short corner to finish.

Ravensdale   (OS Ref 173737)
A magnificently situated, western-facing limestone cliff, Ravensdale dominates the tiny Cressbrook valley and provides high-quality climbs. Popular and extremely pleasant, it is approached from the end of the cul-de-sac road in 10 minutes.

60.1 **Enigma**   HVS   (3c, 5a)
1) 60 ft./18 m. Ascend a chimney groove to a large terrace – belay below the upper wall.   2) 60 ft./18 m. Climb a rib, TR L on a flake crack. Climb a steep wall with difficulty (2 PR).

*60.2 **Frore**   VS   (4c, 4c)
1) 70 ft./21 m. Move on to a ledge and follow a delicate steep groove on the R. Move R and exit at a large tree.   2) 70 ft./21 m. Ascend to a yew on the L and a ledge above. Move R to a groove. Climb it 15 ft./4 m. and move R over an o/H to a ledge, step R and finish direct.

*60.3 **Ploy**   VS   (4c, 4b, 4c)
1) 80 ft./24 m. Move on to a ledge and L into a steep crack. Ascend it and move L over steep rock to a large stance.
2) 45 ft./14 m. Up the crack to a yew and TR R to a belay below a groove.   2) 40 ft./12 m. Climb the groove and step L (PR), climbing direct to the top.

59   Rubicon Wall, Water-cum-Jolly

60.4 **Purple Haze HVS (5a, 5a)
1) 80 ft./24 m. Climb R of a flake to an overhung groove, up it (PR) and up steep but easier rocks to the large ledge on the L. 2) 70 ft./21 m. Climb the crack to the yew (as 60.3). Climb the wall above to a bulge (PR on L) and up a shallow groove.

***60.5 **Mephistopheles** HVS (5a, 5b)
1) 80 ft./24 m. A steep wall leads to a break. Step R and climb the crack (1 PR). Either move R or continue direct before ascending to the large ledge. 2) 70 ft./21 m. A groove goes up from the ledge. Climb it to a bulge. Pull over and climb a steep crack above.

60.5A **Bullets** HVS (5a, 5b)
1) 80 ft./24 m. Start 6 ft./2 m. L of 60.4. Climb shallow groove to break, step up and L on to a thin flake which leads L to the arête. Climb this and over an O/H to belay. 2) 65 ft./20 m. Climb the L arête to a PR, climb a fist-jamming crack above.

60.5B **Mealystopheles VS (4c, 4c)
1) 70 ft./21 m. Start L of the toe of the buttress, below a shallow chimney. Climb up to the chimney and up grooves to a stance. 2) 80 ft./24 m. Climb the slab on the L to a scoop, then move up R to join the finishing crack of 60.5.

*60.6 **Mealybugs** VS (4c, 4b)
1) 70 ft./21 m. Follow the chimney crack and groove to its end and ascend to a ledge out on the R. 2) 80 ft./24 m. Climb the slab on the L to an easier angled area at 30 ft./9 m. TR L and finish up a crack.

***60.7 **Via Vita** HVS (4c, 5b)
1) 85 ft./26 m. Climb a flake on the R and a loose wall to a ledge. Continue up the fine v-groove to a stance (thread B). 2) 75 ft./23 m. A slab on the L is quitted at 20 ft./6 m. by a swing R to a small ledge (PR in place). Climb the exposed crack free throughout. The hanging groove below the final crack is harder (E1, 5c).

60   Ravensdale Crag, Cressbrook

***60.8 **Medusa**   VS   (4b, 4b, 4b)
  1) 60 ft./18 m. Climb a flake on the R and a loose wall to a ledge. Belay on the R.   2) 30 ft./9 m. Jam a fine crack to a small stance (Thread B).   3) 60 ft./18 m. A slab on the L is climbed to a groove on the L. Exit up this.

60.9 **Delusor   VS   (4b, 5a, 4c)
  1) 40 ft./12 m. Climb the wall from L to R to a ledge below the groove, or climb a fierce groove direct to this point.
  2) 105 ft./32 m. Climb the crack direct, using the R wall to overcome the o/H, and reach the upper exit crack. (As for 60.8)

*60.10 **Hades**   HVS   (4c, 5b)
  1) 45 ft./14 m. Climb the wall and shallow groove to a ledge. Continue up a groove (1 PR) and move L to a ledge. Belay on the L.   2) 105 ft./32 m. A flaky crack leads to a pillar. Overcome a bulge (1 PR) and pass a ledge. Follow a steep groove to a tree and finish by the L-hand groove above, until a final exit L.

***60.11 **Conclusor**   HVS   (4c, 5b)
  1) 45 ft./14 m. Follow the corner to a ledge and block.
  2) 105 ft./32 m. Move R and climb the groove to a ledge (PR). Ascend past a bulge and exit R with difficulty. Step back L above to a final crack.

60.12 **Myopia**   HVS   (4c, 5a)
  1) 45 ft./14 m. Shallow grooves are followed up the buttress front to a grass bank. Up it to belay below the tower (PB).   2) 70 ft./21 m. Pull very steeply over the first bulge and climb a blank section (2 PR) to a very steep crack. Follow it to the top.

60.13 **Hi-Fi**   70 ft./21 m.   VS   (4c)
  Climb a shallow groove and go R to flakes. Continue via an obvious corner on good rock.

60.14 **The Wick**   80 ft./24 m.   VS   (4b)
  Climb to the corner and follow it, in part on the R arête, before a steep finish.

*60.15 **Sneck**   80 ft./24 m.   HVS   (5a)
A difficult wall leads to the bulge. With 1 PR, pull into the
upper groove and follow it to an exit R.

60.16 **Malpossessed   80 ft./24 m.   HVS   (5a)
Up the arête and R below the O/H. Enter the groove on the L (1
PR) and bridge the second groove on the L very steeply to easier
ground and a final steep move on to the grass.

60.16A **Wilt**   65 ft./20 m.   E5   (6b)
Climb a roof to a tiny shelf and TR R to steep crack. Climb this
with difficulty.

*60.16B **Cut Loose or Fly**   65 ft./20 m.   E3   (5c)
Start R of the corner. Climb the steep crack on to the wall and
move R to a shallow niche. Climb the wall direct to finish.

***60.17 **Tria**   60 ft./18 m.   S   (4b)
Bridge the excellent corner.

60.18 **Ash Crack   50 ft./15 m.   S   (4a)
Jam the polished crack past the ash.

60.19 **Impendent   60 ft./18 m.   VS   (4c)
Jam the fine crack past the O/H and finish up steep rock on
moderately sound holds.

60.20 **Amain   70 ft./21 m.   VS   (4c)
An initial bulge in the crack is strenuous, leading to a corner.
Exit R at a ledge, with some difficulty.

***60.21 **Gymnic**   70 ft./21 m.   VS   (4c)
Steep cracks lead into a groove (PR). An excellent corner
provides a suitable finish.

60.21A **Scorpion**   70 ft./21 m.   HVS   (5b)
Start 6 ft./2 m. R of a groove and 15 ft./4 m. L of 60.21. Attain a
niche, move R and climb a flake to the arête above.

** *60.22* **Beachcomber**   70 ft./21 m.   HVS   (5a)
Climb the front face of the tower, moving R at a small o/H, then
back R to the arête, before finishing direct up the centre.

Stoney Middleton   (OS Ref 218758–227757)
The dusty quarry-scarred defile has become the forcing ground
of extreme limestone climbing in Derbyshire, with rock climbs
as hard technically as any in Britain. A rock climber's
apocalyptic vision of the wasteland, it is perhaps fitting that it
attracts devotees of the ferocious, steep and uncompromising;
but there are climbs of all standards, the rocks face south and
there is the attraction of nearness to the A623 and to Eric's Café
and the social life of village pubs central to Derbyshire clmbing
since the early Sixties.

Garage Buttress   (OS Ref 227757)
The R edge of the buttress gives.

* *61.1* **Aquiline**   VS   (4c, 5a)
1) 100 ft./30 m. Ascend the wall to a ledge and TR R (PR) to a
wall. Climb to a tree and TR R round the arête to easier
climbing to a terrace ledge.   2) 50 ft./15 m. A very steep wall
is climbed past a PR into a shallow groove.

** *61.2* **Evasor**   VS   (4c, 4c)
1) 60 ft./18 m. The R rib of the scoop is reached by easy rocks
and climbed to the hanging tree (1 PR near top).   2) 90 ft./
27 m. Move up to the rake. TR L for 30 ft./9 m. 2 PR and enter a
short groove. Exit R then move up and R to a steep finish.

*** *61.3* **Little Plum**   E6   (7a, 6c)
1) 30 ft./9 m. Scramble to a tree belay.   2) 60 ft./18 m. Ascend
the overhanging scoop on the R and a wall above to a flake.
Climb to the rake.   3) 40 ft./12 m. TR L and ascend the roof at
its widest point. Climb from the niche above. The whole climb
is free.

61–64   Stoney Middleton Crag

**61.4 Rippemoff HVS (3a, 5b, 5a)

1) 40 ft./12 m. Climb steep grass and rock to the rock wall
(PB).   2) 55 ft./17 m. A loose wall leads to a niche. Exit to the
rake with difficulty (1 PR). TR R to a stance (PB).   3) 55 ft./
17 m. Move L and pull over a bulge (1 PR). Climb the steep wall
(PR) to a final cunning L-stepping exit.

* V Helicon 55 ft./17 m. E2 (5b)

An alternative to (3). Move L to the corner shallow groove.
Climb it with difficulty (1 PR to start and 1 PR at 25 ft./8 m.).

***61.5 Pendulum VS (4c, 4c, 5a)

Start at the platform at the east end of the buttress and about
80 ft./24 m. up the crag, reached by 61.1 or a TR from the gully
on the R.   1) 80 ft./24 m. Follow the rake to an uncomfortable
sitting stance, with 2 PR, PB.   2) 130 ft./40 m. TR L across a
groove and past another cutting through the rock above (PR).
TR into a corner below a roof (2 PR) and past an arête. Follow
the rake to a stance on the saddle (several PR, PB).   3) 100
ft./30 m. TR easily to the end of a shelf (PR). Continue with
difficulty (3 PR) until a descent from the last of these leads to a
grass ledge below. Belay on a tree.

*61.6 Atropos VS (4a, 4c)

1) 60 ft./18 m. A rib L of the scoop is reached by easy rocks and
climbed to the hanging tree (1 PR near top).   2) 100 ft./30 m.
Follow the TR L from the tree at hand level for 10 ft./3 m., then
at foot level for 35 ft./11 m. to a small ledge. Semi-hand-TR for
25 ft./8 m. (3 PR) to a good ledge in a groove. Escape via 61.4 or
by abseil.

**61.7 Compositae Groove HVS (3a, 5a)

1) 90 ft./27 m. Climb mixed grass and rock to a tree.   2) 60
ft./18 m. Climb the wall to the groove and up to the O/H (PR).
Move L and ascend to a yew.

*61.8 Ticket to the Underworld E2 (5c)

1) 90 ft./27 m. Climb a grassy wall to a tree belay L of
61.7.   2) 60 ft./18 m. Take the wall L of 61.7 to a break and
ledge on the R. Move L and over an O/H (PR) to flakes which are
climbed to the top.

Windyledge Buttress   (OS Ref 225757)

***62.1 **Aurora**   VS   (4c, 4c)

1) 100 ft./30 m. Climb easy ledges R of the arête and up an awkward box corner to a ledge on the R. Move L on to a shelf ending on the arête and follow it. Climb the nose direct to a terrace (not well protected).   2) 70 ft./21 m. Go round the corner to an obvious groove crack. Climb direct to near the top, where it steepens, and step L to the altar. Move up the edge on to a larger shelf and the top.

V Aurora Arête   70 ft./21 m.   HVS   (5a)

An alternative to pitch (2). Climb the L side of the arête to a groove (1 PR) and small roof. Overcome this and continue direct to the free-standing altar, with 1 PR before the last bulge.

*62.1A **Menopause**   E5   (6a, 6c)

1) 50 ft./15 m. From the R end of Windy Ledge, climb the shallow groove to o/H of 62.2, then to the stance of 62.2
2) 30 ft./9 m. Climb direct from the cave to a bulge. Enter a groove (crux) and continue direct.

***62.2 **Our Father**   E3   (6a, 5a)

1) 45 ft./14 m. Pull over an o/H and layback a flake until it is possible to step R (PR). Move R (2nd PR). Move up past the 'thread' o/H to the cave (PB).   2) 35 ft./11 m. TR R for 10 ft./3 m. and climb the groove.

V 2) Hysterectomy   E4   (6c)

Takes the shallow groove R of the cave belay (PR), 35 ft./11 m.

***62.3 **Scoop Wall**   E2   (5b, 5b)

1) 50 ft./15 m. Enter a sentry box and climb the bulge above by layaway moves into the crack above, the last move on to the TR line being most awkward. Move R to the cave (PB).
2) 30 ft./9 m. Move L to the corner and reach a crack on the L, which is climbed.

***62.4 **Windhover**   HVS   (5b, 4c)
1) 45 ft./14 m. Pull over the initial bulge and climb L of the arête for 15 ft./4 m. Move R and ascend to a good ledge on the L. PB.   2) 35 ft./11 m. Go round the arête and across to a corner, finishing by the tree.

V.1 Windhover Direct   35 ft./11 m.   (5a)
An alternative to pitch (2). Follow a crack and continue direct.

*** **V.2 Armaggedon**   45 ft./14 m.   HVS   (5b)
an alternative pitch (2). TR L 10 ft./3 m. to a corner (PR), ascend to a 2nd PR and step L to a traversing line. Ascend a crack over the O/H to finish.

***62.5 **The Flakes**   100 ft./30 m.   HVS   (5b)
Pull over the initial bulge and climb L of the arête for 15 ft./4 m. Move up to a PR and swing L on to a line under roofs. Follow this to a final O/H and step L. It is possible to belay on the L and escape via the groove (4c), but better to continue over the O/H on to flakes above, which lead to the final crack.

***62.6 **Special K**   85 ft./24 m.   E3   (6a)
Climb the L-slanting flake, go up the wall a few feet and move R to a groove (PR). Climb the groove and wall to the O/H (Thread). Pull round the O/H into a groove, PR. Step L and then go diagonally R to the top.

62.7 **Kingdom Come**   80 ft./24 m.   E3   (6a)
Free-climb the crack and reach a foot-ledge (PB possible). Pull into the final groove and finish more easily.

62.7A **Circe   80 ft./24 m.   E5   (6a)
Go up the lower wall to a groove and climb it to a bolt R. Move R to a block then R again. Climb a bulge and groove.

62.8 **Dies Irae   80 ft./24 m.   E2   (5b)
Follow the thin crack direct over the bulge and on up the wall (PRS).

62.7   *Neil Foster on Kingdom Come, Stoney Middleton*

62.9 **Inquisitor**   79 ft./21 m.   E1   (5c)
A short wall leads to the bulge. Climb it (1 PR) and climb the flake, exiting L on to grass. Finish by a chimney.

62.10 **Tower of Babel**   110 ft./33 m.   HVS   (5a)
Climb the wall to the L of the Tower (PR). TR R into the groove in the Tower front and climb it, deviating to the R a little, to the summit (1 PR).

***62.11 **Sin**   VS   (2a, 4c)
1) 25 ft./8 m. Climb a chimney, PB on R.   2) 75 ft./23 m. climb the R-hand groove to a horizontal break. Continue with a little more difficulty.

** **V1 Lucy Simmons**   E2   (2a, 5b)
2) 75 ft./23 m. Climb the R-hand groove to the horizontal break, move R on to the buttress front and climb it direct.

** **V2 Glory Road**   VS   (4c)
2) 70 ft./21 m. Climb the groove L of 62.11 (polished).

62.12 **Babylon Bypass**   S   (4a)
1) 25 ft./8 m. Climb the chimney to a stance on the R.
2) 55 ft./17 m. Continue up the chimney until it ends. Make a steep move on to grass.

62   Stoney Middleton, Windyledge Buttress and the Tower of Babel

***62.13 **Alcasan**   E2   (4c, 4c, 5b, 5a, 5b, 5c, 5b)
The TR of Windyledge Buttress.   1) 100 ft./30 m. Climb easy
ledges R of the arête and up an awkward box corner to a ledge
on the R. Move L on to a shelf ending on the arête and follow it.
Climb the nose direct to a terrace.   2) 55 ft./17 m. Go round
the corner to an obvious groove crack. Climb direct to a point
near the where it steepens, and step L to the altar. PB.
3) 35 ft./11 m. TR L to a groove and continue to the cave of
62.3 (2 PR).   4) 45 ft./14 m. Step into the corner and descend
6 ft./2 m. TR black loose rock to the arête (PR). PB and ledge
above.   5) 50 ft./15 m. Descend 15 ft./4 m. and TR under the
black roofs (1 PR to start, 1 PR at end) to a stance in a groove
(PB).   6) 40 ft./12 m. Go L and descend into a groove. TR L to
belay in a crack (PB).   7) 115 ft./35 m. Go L and climb the
groove. Reach the final wall. TR this with difficulty (2 PR) to a
groove. Exit L on to grass and finish up an awkward chimney.

63.1 **Mineshaft**   80 ft./24 m.   M   (2a)
Ascend or descend the vast chimney.

63.2 **Fe Fi Fo Fum   60 ft./18 m.   HVS   (5a)
Climb a little groove and TR R to a crack, which is followed
until an escape on to the arête near the top.

V Beanstalk Erect   60 ft./18 m.   E2   (5c)
Climb the arête to join 63.2. 1 PR at 20 ft./6 m.

***63.2A **Bitter Fingers**   80 ft./24 m.   E4   (6a)
Climb steeply up the wall to the break (PR). Step L and follow a
vague crack to the top.

***63.3 **Dead Banana Crack**   HVS   (5b)
1) 90 ft./27 m. The wall is climbed to the crack. Enter the crack
and climb to the quartzite frieze. TR L to belay on Wallop
(63.4V). PB.   2) 40 ft./12 m. Go back to the tree, stand on it
and climb the wall going L, with difficulty.

63.2A Svetoslav on Bitter Fingers, Stoney Middleton

63.4 Froth VS (4a, 4c)
1) 60 ft./18 m. Climb the corner. PB. 2) 50 ft./15 m. Go R along the quartzite frieze, passing a tree to the niche (PR). Ascend the steep wall.

V Wallop S (4b)
2) 20 ft./6 m. Go into the corner, exit L and ascend to the top.

63.5 Golden Gate VS (4c, 4b)
1) 60 ft./18 m. Climb the crack and groove, lay-backing an awkward O/H. PB on L. 2) 60 ft./18 m. TR the foot-ledge to the L to the block. Swing on to this and climb the arête on the L.

63.6 Pickpocket E3 (6a, 4c)
1) 65 ft./20 m. Climb 15 ft./4 m. up the wall to a thin crack. Attain a shallow groove and an exit R at the top on to the wall. Climb pockets to a good ledge. Leave the L end and reach a horizontal break. Step R and use undercuts to reach a ledge. Nut belays. 2) 45 ft./14 m. TR R to the corner, climb up a few feet and TR L to a crack. Climb it.

63.7 Medusa 80 ft./24 m. HVS (5a)
Climb the wall to a tree stump. Move steeply R into the L-hand crack and jam it (strenuous) past an O/H to a standing place. Move slightly R and back L on to the ledge.

63.8 Wee Doris 60 ft./18 m. E3 (5c)
Climb a shallow scoop for 15 ft./4 m. and move R to a ledge below a thin crack. Move over the bulge and climb the ferocious upper wall by blind moves.

63.9 Sickle 40 ft./12 m. HVS (5b)
Climb a shallow groove and move L with difficulty to finish.

63.10 Thrutch HVS (5a)
1) 30 ft./9 m. Climb the corner to a stance (PB). 2) 35 ft./11 m. Climb the corner to a ledge, move R and mantelshelf on to it with difficulty.

63.3   *Dead Banana Crack, Froth Bay, Stoney Middleton. Jack Street*

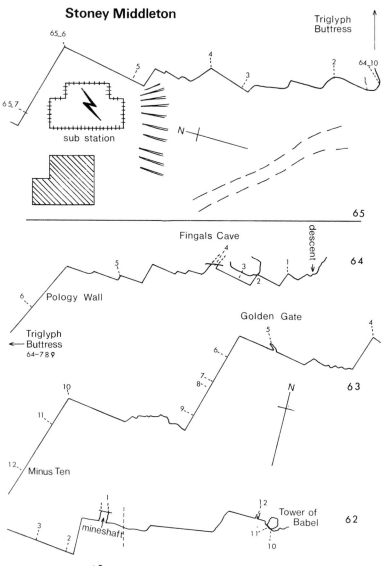

Stoney Middleton

Triglyph
Buttress

65_6

5

4

3

2

64_10

65_7

sub station

N

65

Fingals Cave

descent

64

5

4

3

1

6

Pology Wall

2

Golden Gate

Triglyph
Buttress
64-7 8 9

5

4

6

10

7

8

63

11

9

12

Minus Ten

mineshaft

Tower of
Babel

3

2

12

11

10

62

63

*63.11 **Cointreau**   VS   (4d)
1) 30 ft./9 m. Ascend the polished crack to a ledge (PB).
2) 35 ft./11 m. Continue steeply up the upper corner, escaping L.

63.12 **Minus Ten   50 ft./15 m.   VS   (4c)
Climb the steep jamming-crack.

*64.1 **Parachute**   40 ft./12 m.   S   (3c)
Climb the corner, passing a tree stump.

***64.2 **The Pearly Gates**   VS   (4c, 4c)
1) 70 ft./21 m. Climb the corner to the top (PR). Move R to a large ledge.   2) 70 ft./21 m. TR L on to the buttress front and climb into a little groove (PR). Climb this and the bulge, moving L to finish.

64.3 **The White Knight**   VD   (3a, 3a, 2b)
1) 50 ft./15 m. Climb the middle of the face to a move R on to a good ledge. Tree belay on L.   2) 20 ft./6 m. Overcome a bulge awkwardly and move L to a tree belay.   3) 30 ft./9 m. Exit up the gully.

64.4 **Fingal's Cave**   VD   (3b, 2c)
1) 55 ft./17 m. Chimney up the far inside of the cave and through a hole.   2) 40 ft./12 m. Climb the chimney. Do not take a route nearer the cave mouth (VS).

*64.5 **Minestrone**   90 ft./27 m.   HS   (4b)
Climb a little groove to the O/H and move L into a corner. Climb the corner, with an awkward mantelshelf. TR R to easier climbing.

V Asparagus   90 ft./27 m.   S   (4a)
The corner can be climbed direct from the base.

64.6 **Pology Wall   HVS   (5a)
1) 55 ft./17 m. Climb the wall at its centre, with difficult moves at two-thirds height (1–2 PR usually in place). Step L and belay on grass ledges.   2) 30 ft./9 m. TR R to a shallow groove and climb the O/H, then move R to a crack.

Stoney Middleton – The Tryglyph

64.7 **Morning Crack**   65 ft./20 m.   S   (4a)
Climb the ʀ-hand crack.

64.8 **What the Hell   85 ft./26 m.   VS   (4c)
The central crack is climbed, mainly by jamming.

***64.9 **How the Hell**   85 ft./26 m.   VS   (4c)
The wide crack proves awkward in places but gives excellent climbing.

64.10 **Little Capucin**   HVS   (3a, 5a)
1) 60 ft./18 m. Ascend the face to a ledge ʀ of the final wall.   2) 40 ft./12 m. Move ʟ to a niche. Pull over the bulge and follow a crack to the top. Loose.

Stoney Middleton Quarry

65.1 **Mortuary Steps   HVS   (2c, 5a)
1) 60 ft./18 m. Go up to a tree and climb the groove behind to a small ledge under the o/ʜ (ᴘʙ).   2) 40 ft./12 m. Step ʟ and enter the groove with difficulty. Climb it (ᴘʀ at mid-height).

V1 Morgue   E2   (5b)
2) 45 ft./14 m. Tʀ further ʟ. Pull over the bulge (1 ᴘʀ). Climb the wall above (1 ᴘʀ).

V2 Speed Kills   E4   (6a)
2) 45 ft./14 m. Pull over the bulge (1 ᴘʀ) and climb the steep wall.

*65.2 **Drainpipe Groove**   VS   (4b, 4c)
1) 60 ft./18 m. Climb the clean corner to a stance on the ʟ (ᴘʙ).   2) 40 ft./12 m. Climb shelves to the fine upper crack.

65   *Craig Smith on Helmut Schmitt, Stoney Middleton Quarry*

65.3 **The Slurper HVS (5b, 5b)
1) 50 ft./15 m. Climb the wall to a thin crack and follow it to a stance. PB. 2) 50 ft./15 m. Move L into the crack and climb it, to a niche. Exit L.

*65.4 **Acrophobia** VS (4c, 4a)
1) 70 ft./21 m. Climb the corner by bridging to a final steep bulge. Belay on a tree. 2) 20 ft./6 m. Climb a corner on the L.

65.5 **John Peel** 80 ft./24 m. E1 (5b)
Climb the thin crack to an O/H and pull over it into a groove. Climb to the horizontal break, step L and pull over it into a groove. Climb to the horizontal break, step L and climb loose flakes to a short corner to finish.

***65.6 **Brown Corner** 80 ft./24 m. HVS (5a)
Up the R wall into the corner. Jam the steep crack and climb it direct.

65.6A **Oliver 75 ft./23 m. E3 (5c)
Climb the groove 15 ft./4 m. L of 65.6 to a bulge. Move L and climb up to a break. Move R and up to an overlap. Move L and finish direct.

65.7 **Jasper 70 ft./21 m. E3 (5c)
Start 15 ft./4 m. R of the arête and climb the thin cracks for 30 ft./9 m. Reach a layback flake and final steep quartz wall.

West Stoney Middleton (OS Ref 215759)

66.1 **Swan Song** 70 ft./21 m. VS (4b)
Either climb the flakes direct or climb the wall on the R to them. Follow the flakes until it is possible to TR to the arête on the R. A broken wall leads to a final groove.

66.2 **Spiron** VS (4c, 4c)
1) 60 ft./18 m. From the L side of the buttress go up a few feet and TR R to a PR. Continue R by a second PR to a ledge. PB.
2) 25 ft./8 m. TR L to the arête and climb it to finish.

65 Stoney Middleton Quarry

Harpur Hill Quarry – Papacy Buttress

(OS Ref 062707)

Though access is forbidden, the Papacy Buttress has several climbs of unusual character. The cliff is approached across the fields behind the Harpur Hill Institute, two miles south of Buxton. (15–20 minutes from the road.)

***67.1 **Seven Deadly Sins**   VS   (4b, 4c)

1) 40 ft./12 m. Climb the corner to a bulge and swing round the arête to a small sloping ledge. A jamming-crack leads to a slab stance. Chock belays.   2) 60 ft./18 m. Tr L to a ledge, ascend (PR), and TR R to a depression (PR). Continue R and climb a groove of precarious rock.

67.2 **Lust**   90 ft./27 m.   VS   (4c)

Climb a wide overhanging crack to a scoop, bridge up and swing R at an o/h (PR) and finish by a scoop.

67.3 **Seven Deadly Virtues**   HVS   (5b, 4c)

1) 60 ft./18 m. Move up the crack of 67.2 and TR R to a hanging groove in the face. Climb it (PR) to a small o/h and step R to a ledge with difficulty (PB).   2) 40 ft./12 m. Go R to a groove (PR) and step R to a detached block. Slant back R to finish (stake belay).

Aldery Cliff – Earl Sterndale   (OS Ref 097663)

A compact, sheltered cliff of unusual quarried limestone is situated half a mile south-east of Earl Sterndale on the Crowdecote road. It is 25 yds/23 m. from the road. The cliff is rarely crowded.

*68.1 **Clothesline**   S   (4a, 3b)

1) 50 ft./15 m. Climb the corner to a ledge.
2) 50 ft./15 m. Up the steep wall on the R.

*68.1A **Surface Plate**   100 ft./30 m.   VS   (4c)
Climb the thin crack up the centre of the slab and finish up
cracks in the wall above.

68.2 **Broken Toe**   VS   (4b, 3b)
Climb the vague R-hand crack and slab to a tree (belay).
2) 50 ft./15 m. Move R and climb a crack. Beyond a PR, finish
up a loose bulge.

68.3 **Ash Tree Slab**   VD   (3a, 3b)
1) 40 ft./12 m. From a small corner move R to a ledge and
follow cracks to a tree.   2) 40 ft./12 m. Move on to the arête
and climb it.

68.4 **Carmen**   80 ft./24 m.   VS   (4b)
Climb a steep wall past a sapling and thread to diagonal cracks
and steep moves to reach a tree. Finish more easily.

68.5 **The Cardinal**   60 ft./18 m.   VS   (4b)
A crack leads to a slanting ledge in the corner. Climb the
awkward corner to a large ledge to finish up grassy rocks.

*68.6 **The Arête**   VS   (4c)
Climb the obvious L edge of Cardinal Corner.

Dovedale   (OS Ref 152513–141539)
A beautiful and meandering valley, narrow and enlivened by a
fine rapid-flowing river, Dovedale has become a major
attraction for climbers during the last three decades. The
pinnacles are unique in Derbyshire, and some of the face climbs
are of high quality.
   The climbing is concentrated between Milldale in the north
and Thorpe Cloud, a distance of about three miles. All climbs
can be reached in less than one hour from the road by the valley
footpath.

69   Ravenstor, Dovedale

Dovedale

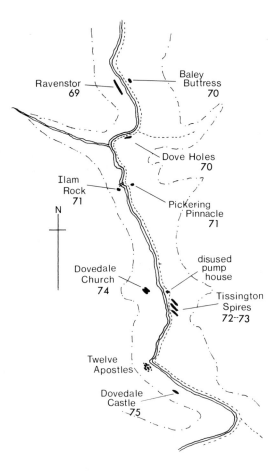

Ravenstor
69

Baley
Buttress
70

Dove Holes
70

Ilam
Rock
71

Pickering
Pinnacle
71

N

disused
pump
house

Dovedale
Church
74

Tissington
Spires
72–73

Twelve
Apostles

Dovedale
Castle
75

Ravenstor   (OS Ref 142538)

Perhaps the most important single cliff in the valley, with steep high-standard climbing. It is reached in 15 minutes from Milldale, going south.

*69.1 **Parrot Face**   HVS   (4b, 5a)
  1) 70 ft./21 m. Climb a v-groove in line with the L-hand crack and step R to belay below the R-hand crack.   2) 65 ft./20 m. The crack is steep with good jams to an O/H. Pull over this with difficulty.

***69.2 **Venery**   HVS   (4b, 5a)
  1) 70 ft./21 m. Climb a v-groove in line with the L-hand crack and move up to a belay R of it.   2) 80 ft./24 m. Move L into the crack and ascend it direct.

69.3 **Brown's Blunder   S   (4a, 4a)
  1) 60 ft./18 m. Take a diagonal break L of the dirty gully, with a hard move to escape it to a belay ledge.   2) 50 ft./15 m. Up a ramp on the L to steep grass.

69.4 **Central Wall   E2   (5c, 5a)
  1) 70 ft./21 m. Up a crack to a ledge. Make steep difficult moves to reach a further hard section and the traversing line. Step R to belay. PB.   2) 40 ft./12 m. (6a, 5a). Either climb L crack above stance, or move L and follow a steep groove and flake to a grassy finish.

69.5 **Aquarius   HVS   (5b, 5a)
  1) 100 ft./30 m. Go 15 ft./4 m. up 69.3. Climb the fierce crack R of the thread to a stance. (PB).   2) 50 ft./15 m. Continue up the crack and over steep grass.

69.6 **Raven   HVS   (5b, 5b)
  1) 75 ft./23 m. Follow the steep crack to join the rake of 69.3. Move up to a stance.   2) 55 ft./17 m. Climb the groove above and move steeply R to a block. Finish up and R.

***69.7 **Left-hand Route**   HVS   (5b, 5a)
  1) 80 ft./24 m. Climb the diedre, with 1 PR high up.
  2) 50 ft./15 m. Continue up a ramp on the L, and over steep grass.

69.7A Temptress   E4   (6a, 5c, 4a)
1) 65 ft./20 m. Start at a scoop just L of 69.7. Move up and R (PR) to a good hold. Move steeply up and L to belay on 69.8.   2) 50 ft./15 m. Follow 69.8 to the O/H. TR R to a P, then climb a crack to a ledge.   3) 40 ft./12 m. Go straight up a grassy ramp.

69.8 Southern Rib   HVS   (5a, 5a, 4a)
1) 55 ft./17 m. Climb a bulging crack to its end and move L by a loose flake into a groove. Exit L to a small stance (1 PR).
2) 60 ft./18 m. Follow the slanting groove through O/HS and step L into a steep groove. Go up 10 ft./3 m. and move R to grass ledges (PB).   2) 50 ft./15 m. Go straight up.

69.9 Girdle Traverse   HVS   (4b, 4c, 4c, 5a)
1) 55 ft./17 m. Up the gully to a tree and TR R to a ledge. PB.
2) 55 ft./17 m. Follow the slanting groove through O/HS and step R before moving round a corner and down to a ledge.   3) 80 ft./24 m. TR 69.4 by obvious ledges and lines of holds to the gully. Tree belay beyond it.   4) 70 ft./21 m. Descend the arête 5 ft./2 m. and follow a line of holds into the crack of 69.2 – climb this direct.

Bailey Buttress   (OS Ref 142539)
Opposite Ravenstor, on the path side of the river, there is an isolated and peculiarly ridged buttress.

70.1A Flying Blackberry   E3   (6a, 4c)
1) 75 ft./23 m. Climb into groove on L and go up to a roof. Follow crack R. Continue to L.   2) 70 ft./21 m. Climb the corner to a ledge and finish up a diagonal fault.

70.1 The Claw   HVS   (5a, 4c)
1) 70 ft./21 m. Climb the central thin crack to an overhanging chimney and ascend this with difficulty to a stance on the L (PB).
2) 65 ft./20 m. TR R along a break and climb a diagonal fault to the ridge.

70   Bailey Buttress

**70.1B Claw Direct   80 ft./24 m.   HVS   (5b)

Take the obvious chimney groove to an easing at the chockstone. Either move R to join 70.1 or finish direct (5c).

Dove Holes   (OS Ref 142235)

The larger Dove Hole forms a large roof.

**70.2 The Bat   A3   (4a)

1) 80 ft./24 m. Free-climb the back pillar to a bolt. A total of 10 bolts and several pegs are used to overcome the roof. A short wall leads to a belay ledge.   2) 40 ft./12 m. Free-climb steep rock and grass (10 P, 10 bolts).

70.2C Pumping Iron   80 ft./24 m.   E4   (6b)

Takes the large overlap in the wall between the two Dove Holes. Climb from L to R to a PR. Move 6 ft./2 m. R and pull over the overlap before continuing to the top.

70.2B Police and Thieves   60 ft./18 m.   E4   (6a)

Follow 70.2A for 15 ft./4 m., then go L to a flake. Pass 1 PR and a bulge and continue up the top wall.

*70.2A The Umpire   60 ft./18 m.   E2   (5c)

Start at a shallow groove R of the cave. Climb the wall and groove to a ledge. Go L to a flake and finish direct.

The Ilam Rock Area   (OS Ref 142531)

Where the valley narrows to a gorge, two fine pinnacles dominate its entrance, one on either bank of the river. They and the less spectacular buttresses behind Pickering Tor give unique limestone climbing.

70.2   The Bat, Dove Holes, Dovedale

Ilam Rock

***71.1 **The White Edge, Easter Island** E2 (5c)
Start from ledge on R arête of the main face of the pinnacle.
Move round the arête to the R and climb the face to a ledge.
Climb a crack on the L and the arête until steep moves lead L
and up a finishing groove.

71.1A **The Gladiator 80 ft./24 m. E3 (6a)
Start 15 ft./4 m. R of the col below a steep crack. Strenuous
moves lead past a hole to a crack. Climb this to the top and
move L to a ledge. Finish up and R around the arête to join the
main face (crux).

*71.2 **The Groove** 70 ft./21 m. E1 (5c)
Ascend the overhanging groove to a small tree and continue
direct. Descend by abseil.

*71.2A **Wong Edge** 70 ft./21 m. E2 (5c)
From the col, climb the o/H crack, moving R at the bulge.
Either finish direct or step L to an easing of angle.

Pickering Tor

*71.3 **The Flake** 65 ft./20 m. E1 (5b)
Climb a fierce crack on the L side of the flake, starting from the
col, c (see page 000). From a ledge, climb the face round the
corner to the top. Descend by abseil.

71.4 **Pickering's Overhang 65 ft./20 m. E1 (5b)
Tr L from the col, below 71.3, to the groove and ascend to the
o/H. Surmount this and climb the upper wall (2 PR) to the top.
Descend by abseil.

71.1   *The White Edge, Easter Island*

Pickering Wall

**71.5 Thunderball   HVS   (5b, 4c)

1) 50 ft./15 m. Climb 10 ft./3 m. up the groove and TR R across the wall to a foothold (1 PR). Move up to a shallow groove (PB).

2) 40 ft./12 m. Climb the corner and move L (PR) before climbing direct to a tree.

71.5A Final Witness   60 ft./18 m.   E1   (5b)

Start as for 71.5, but climb direct up the groove and pocketed wall above to a ledge. Move R and finish up a short chimney.

Overhang Buttress

71.6 Beginner's Luck   70 ft./21 m.   S   (4a, 4a)

Climb the slab from the nose of the buttress, or the overhanging layback crack. Go up a corner and L by an O/H to a ledge (PB). Go R under an O/H to finish up a short corner.

Watchblock Tower

71.7 Watchblock Direct   125 ft./38 m.   HVS   (5a)

Climb the wall (50 ft./15 m. R of the tunnel) going R to a bulge. Move R and climb the bulge. Step R and go L to easier slabs; climb them direct just L of the Watchblock.

***71.7A Wall of Straws   125 ft./38 m.   E4   (6b)

From the tunnel L of 71.8, climb the edge to a roof. TR R to smooth groove, go up it to 71.8 and follow it, but go up where it moves L. Go R to the L edge of a slab to finish.

***71.8 Adjudicator Wall   130 ft./40 m.   E3   (5c)

Climb a shallow depression L of the lowest point for 30 ft./9 m. Go diagonally L to a PR and finish up a crack above.

71.3–8   P-Pickering Tor- C-Col; PW-Pickering Wall; OB-Overhang Buttress; W-Watchblock Buttress, Dovedale

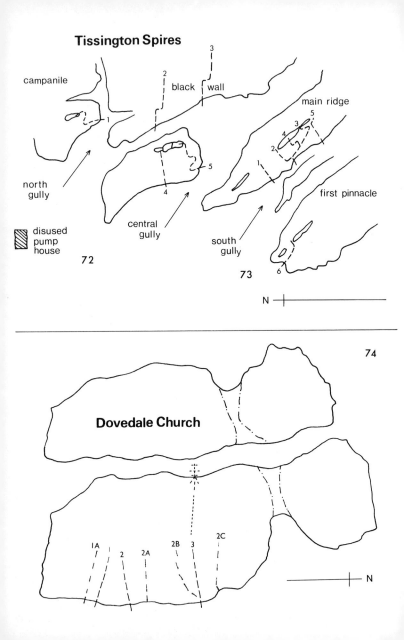

Tissington Spires

campanile

2

3

black wall

north gully

1

disused pump house

72

5

4

central gully

main ridge

4 3 5

2

1

south gully

first pinnacle

6

73

N

74

Dovedale Church

1A

2

2A

2B

3

2C

N

Lower Dovedale   (OS Ref 146521–147515)

Within a distance of less than three-quarters of a mile, there are a series of complex pinnacles and ridges of quite unique character in the Peak, situated on both banks of the river.

Tissington Spires   (OS Ref 146521)

Though conveniently situated near to the tourist path, the Spires pose difficult problems of topography, for they are composed of a series of ridges and semi-detached pinnacles set in trees and divided by overgrown gullies. It is, therefore, to be expected that a little time will be needed to identify climbs. The old pumphouse on the path is the obvious landmark below them, about 20 minutes' walk from the stepping-stones at the south end of Dovedale, near Thorpe Cloud.

* *72.1* **Campanile**   S   (4a, 3c)

1) 50 ft./15 m. Move L and climb a flake on the R before moving L into a corner. Climb this, exciting L (PB).
2) 60 ft./18 m. Go R up a chimney and across a ramp to the edge. Up this, then R again, before ascending to a tree. Abseil or descend the ridge to a yew and TR to the gully.

72.2 **Hortus**   S   (4a, 4a, 4a)

1) 40 ft./12 m. From midway in the gully, climb on to a ledge R of the tree. Move L 10 ft./3 m. and pass an overlap to a ledge before going R to a stance under an O/H.   2) 40 ft./12 m. Go L to a groove and climb it, moving R to a yew.   3) 35 ft./11 m. Go R across a slab to a groove and ascend (PR) to a yew. Scramble to the ridge.

** *72.2A* **Ten Craters of Wisdom**   VS   (4a, 4c)

1) 60 ft./18 m. Climb a wall to a large ledge. Ash belay.
2) 55 ft./17 m. Move 10 ft./3 m. L to a short corner and up to a bulge and slab. Move L to finish.

** *72.3* **Simeon**   VS   (4a, 4c)

1) 60 ft./18 m. Climb a wall past a tree to a large ledge. Belay behind a tree.   2) 50 ft./15 m. Climb the steep wall, TR R and go straight up to a ledge. A hard bulge leads to a yew. Descend on the R.

72.4 **Tormentor**   HVS   (4a, 5a)
1) 60 ft./18 m. Go up gardened rock to a ledge on the R and take the wall to a grass ledge. Go R to belay.   2) 80 ft./24 m. Go back L and climb to a bulge (PR). Climb the crack (PR) and TR R by a horizontal crack (thread in place) to a final groove leading to the col. Abseil descent.

** 72.5 **Silicon**   80 ft./24 m.   VS   (4c)
Climb cleaned rock to a PR. Go L to the base of the crack and climb it direct, exiting R. TR over the summit to the col. Abseil descent.

73.1 **Mandarin**   VS   (4c, 4b)
1) 80 ft./24 m. Climb past trees to R-slanting flakes. Go up a few feet and move L, climbing the face to a hole. Go diagonally R to a little col and tree belay.   2) 50 ft./15 m. Follow the crumbly ridge.

* 73.1A **Brutus**   100 ft./30 m.   E1   (5b)
Climb a thin crack direct to a loose finish at a grassy col. Finish up the ridge or abseil.

*** 73.2 **George**   130 ft./40 m.   HVS   (5b)
TR past trees, with a difficult move, to enter a groove beyond. Go up to a PR. Cross the steep wall on the L (PR) to a steep crack and follow it to a hole. A steep groove above proves difficult.

*** 73.3 **John Peel**   HVS   (5a, 5a, 3a)
1) 100 ft./30 m. TR past trees, until a difficult move can be made into a groove. Go up to a PR. Move R on to a slab and up to a corner. TR R to a small stance. PR.   2) 30 ft./9 m. Climb awkward-sloping shelves on the R to a yew.   3) 50 ft./15 m. Go up L by ledges to finish on the ridge.

73.4 **Black Flip**   E1   (5c), E4   (6c)
1) 70 ft./21 m. From a point 15 ft./4 m. up 73.3, climb a steep vertical break to an overlap and pull over this to the stance of 73.3. PB.   2) 60 ft./18 m. Go up to PR above and TR L. Climb a shallow groove, exit R and finish more easily. Finished direct, it's much harder.

73.3   John Peel, Tissington Spires. Geoff Birtles and Jeff Morgan

** *73.5* **Yew Tree Wall**   E1   (5b, 4c)
    1) 65 ft./20 m. Climb a steep pocketed wall, past a tree, to the large tree. Mantelshelf to a tiny flake. Move R and go up to the yew.   2) 65 ft./20 m. TR a horizontal break R and climb rocks above more easily.

73.6 **Dr Livingstone**   VS   (4b, 4c, 4a)
    1) 70 ft./21 m. Follow the steep corner above the cave and move R to belay.   2) 40 ft./12 m. Climb the corner to the ridge.   3) 70 ft./21 m. Go over the ridge, descend 15 ft./4 m., and TR L to the opposite ridge – up this to the top.

** *73.6A* **Orange Peel**   E3   (5a, 6a, 5b)
    1) 130 ft./40 m. Start well L at a large dead ash tree. Climb steep grass to join the upper of two diagonal breaks. Go along the break to a ledge, then up to a hole and R to a loose grassy finish on the col.   2) 60 ft./18 m. Descend the crack 10 ft./3 m. and TR horizontally R to a good hold. Move up, then R to a sapling and R again to join 73.2. Descend to 73.3 and belay.   3) 120 ft./36 m. Move R and cross above an overlap to hand-TR R into 73.5. Descend a few feet, then move R to a ramp, which is followed to finish.

Dovedale Church   (OS Ref 144523)
These fine pinnacles are situated across the river from the ruined pumphouse.

** *74.1A* **Tales of the Riverbank**   E4   (6a)
    1) 100 ft./30 m. Start below the L arête. Climb the wall and enter the hanging groove. Up this, then L to a crack. Climb up, and L, then back R to finish up a crack.

74.1 **Anaconda**   VS   (4c, 4c)
    1) 60 ft./18 m. Climb the overhanging corner (1 PR at 30 ft./9 m.) past the o/H. Move L to a ledge. PB.   2) 40 ft./12 m. Go R up a crack (1 PR), finally moving L to a grass ledge and a tree. Abseil descent.

74.2 **Phil's Route**   E1   (5c)

1) 70 ft./21 m. Climb a wall and crack to a roof. Overcome this and go up to a block. Above, there is a ledge and PB.
2) 30 ft./9 m. Step down and go L to a crack – climb this. Abseil.

74.2A **Jungle Lord**   E5   (6b)

105 ft./32 m. Follow the old aid route, 'Right Route', using old gear for protection.

74.2B **Wild Country**   E4   (6c)

100 ft./30 m. Go up 74.3 for 10 ft./3 m., then up L. Reach a layback crack and follow it, then TR L round the rib to a slab. Move round the arête and follow cracks to a ledge, and finish up the arête.

74.2C **Amazona**   E5   (6c)

100 ft./30 m. Follow to the top of the crack and continue up the wall on the R.

74.3 **Snakes Alive**   80 ft./24 m.   VS   (4c)

The corner is climbed direct, avoiding the bulge on the L. PB (used for abseil).

74.4 **Quiet Life**   60 ft./18 m.   E2   (5c)

Start R of 74.2 at an undercut scoop and crack. Climb the crack and pull into the scoop. Finish direct.

Dovedale Castle   (OS Ref 147515)

The pinnacle is half a mile north of the Stepping Stones, with a prominent cave.

75.1 **Cat's Eye Corner**   VS   (4c, 4b)

1) 50 ft./15 m. From the L side of the cave, TR R above it to the corner and climb the crack to a ledge on the L.   2) 25 ft./8 m. A move L is made from the top of the corner to a crack. Up this to the top.

75.2 **Castle Crack**   70 ft./21 m.   VS   (5a)

Go R from the cave to a ledge. Go up and R to a rake which leads L to a tree. Move L to the crack. Climb it, with difficulty at the bulge.

Manifold Valley   (OS Ref 096561–107541)

A beautiful and quiet spot, except on summer Sundays, the Manifold valley has some excellent limestone climbing which, in contrast with nearby Dovedale, is primarily situated on compact cliffs which are easily identifiable. The crags vary in aspect: Thor's Cave frequently remaining cold and damp when Beeston Tor basks in winter sunshine. Access is very awkward without much walking unless private transport is used, a factor which has contributed in the past to slow climbing developments. However, once there, all cliffs can be reached in less than 20 minutes.

Ossams Crag   (OS Ref 096554)

***76.1   **Cummerbund**   VS   (4a, 4b)

1) 75 ft./23 m. From the fence, ascend direct to a groove and pull over a bulge to grassy rock. Belay below the tree.
2) 65 ft./20 m. TR R into a fault below O/HS and follow it to ledges beyond a black niche (PB).   3) 60 ft./18 m. Move R and up, then TR R to a corner (PR). Go up to a break and go R to a bay.   4) 30 ft./9 m. Exit L on easy ground.

76.2 **Conventicle**   HVS   (5a, 5b)

1) 100 ft./30 m. From a tree step L on to a ledge and go L 15 ft./4 m. Climb a wall and go R to a ledge, up a wall and R to a small tree. TR R and then climb direct to the ledges above PB.
2) 60 ft./18 m. Go up the groove R of the belay (as 2) 76.1 and continue direct on loose rock (thread R in position).

76.3 **Steerpike**   E1   (5a, 5b, 4c)
1) 45 ft./14 m. Tʀ a ramp to a crack on the ʟ. Climb it to a sloping ledge ᴘʙ.   2) 60 ft./18 m. Move ʀ 15 ft./4 m. and climb direct to reach a tree. Climb a slab to a ᴘʀ. Move ʟ and climb the wall to the grassy bay.   3) 25 ft./8 m. Climb the steep crack.

Thor's Cave   (OS Ref 098549)
A magnificent crag, cutting through by a giant hole, dominates the valley below Wetton and is both a tourist attraction and an excellent climbing ground. Unfortunately the two do not mix and summer Sunday climbing may be inadvisable.

**77.1   Starlight   VS   (4c, 4b)
1) 85 ft./26 m. Easy rocks ʀ of the cave lead to a ledge. Follow the groove past an awkward bulge to a stance and tree.
2) 65 ft./20 m. Jam the steep crack.

**77.2   Lightning   HVS   (5a, 4c)
1) 10 ft./3 m. Easy rock ʀ of the cave lead to a ledge. Move ʀ and climb the wall slightly ʟ, thenascend direct to a spike. Move ʀ and climb a wall before moving ʟ to a groove. Up this to a flake.   2) 50 ft./15 m. Step ʟ and climb a groove-crack to the top.

*77.3   Slanting Crack   VS   (4c, 4c, 4a)
1) 70 ft./21 m. Start low on the north-west face and climb the wall, going slightly ʀ, before moving round the arête to the stance. (You can reach this point from the gully to the ʀ.)
2) 60 ft./18 m. Ascend the chimney to a bulge. Pull over this (steep) and move up to a terrace.   3) 30 ft./9 m. Go ʀ to a corner and ascend to the top.

**77.4   Tower Crack   HVS   (2b, 5b, 4a)
1) 20 ft./6 m. From West Window Gully, move up to the ledge on the ʀ (ᴘʙ).   2) 60 ft./18 m. Start the steep wall on the ʟ, move back ʀ by a flake to the crack and climb it for 20 ft./6 m. to a ᴘʀ.   3) 45 ft./14 m. Go ʀ and climb a short crack.

77   Thor's Cave, Manifold Valley

***77.5 **West Window Groove**   HVS   (5a, 5a)
1) 35 ft./11 m. Climb the L wall to the top of a pillar (PR or
nut). Make a bridging move into the cave (PB).   2) 60 ft./
18 m. Bridge the groove until it eases into a crack. Go R to
finish.

***77.5A **Tower Direct**   120 ft./36 m.   E3   (5c)
Start from a ledge 15 ft./4 m. up 77.5 on the L, facing in. Climb
the R-hand crack above and move L to follow a widening crack
up to ledges. Climb the corner above to a finish slightly L.

***77.5B **Twilight of the Tired Gods**   E3   (5c, 5b)
1) 50 ft./15 m. From the start of 77.5A, obtain a flake from the
L. Follow it to belay in 77.5.   2) 70 ft./21 m. TR L to a crack,
up it, then L to ledges. Move up to finish by a sharp corner.

77.6 **Kyrie Eleison   A3   A3   VS   (4c)
1) 70 ft./21 m. At the back of the cave, L of the West Window,
is a niche. Up slabs into a niche and peg R to near West
Window. Follow the roof fault and descend to a second fault
leading towards the entrance. At its end, go under a bulge to a
hanging niche. Etrier belay (15 P, 9 bolts).   2) 60 ft./18 m.
Make a difficult reach to a bolt and continue past two threads
to the lip. A few feet above is a stance (10 bolts, 3 P, 4 threads).
3) 100 ft./30 m. Climb grooves above, free. Derbyshire's
biggest roof climb.

Beeston Tor   (OS Ref 107541)
An excellent cliff with almost 30 classic climbs and a sunny aspect,
reached in five minutes from the farm below.

***78.1 **The Thorn**   HVS   (4b, 5a)
1) 90 ft./27 m. Climb the slab to a ledge on the R and move L
into the groove-chimney. Giant thread belays.   2) 70 ft./21 m.
Go L and up the wall. Climb the bulge and a crack (PR in
place). Step L and move up into the vegetated break. Exit L
above.

78.1A **Double Top**   E4   (4a, 6a, 5c)
1) 90 ft./27 m. as for 78.1.   2) 25 ft./8 m. From the L end of the
cave, cross the roof crack and enter the crack above with
difficulty. Belay in groove.   3) 60 ft./18 m. Move R across a
steep wall by a thread. Go straight up to join 78.4, pull over the
bulge using a pocket (PR) and move R to finish on the prow.
A series of fine climbs ascend the wall below the
Thorn cave. A chain allows relayed ascents.

*78.1B **Nocturne**   110 ft./33 m.   VS   (4c)
Follow 78.1 for 40 ft./12 m., TR R to a crack and climb L in the
weakness to the cave.

*78.1C **Pocket Symphony**   E1   (5b)
2) 70 ft./21 m. From a belay at 60 ft./18 m. (thread), go up L to
threads. Climb a fine pocketed wall to the cave.

*78.1D **Deaf Dove**   E1   (5c)
2) 65 ft./20 m. From the same stance, climb the steep wall,
finishing direct over a nose.

*78.1E **Evensong**   HVS   (5b)
2) 65 ft./20 m. Climb a scoop between orange patches and
finish over a bulge.

78.1F **Flying Doctor   E5   (5c, 6b)
1) 120 ft./36 m. Climb the hanging groove L of 78.1, taking a
chimney and O/H above to the crux of 78.1. Climb that and
move R. Belay on 78.1A.   2) 95 ft./29 m. Move R on edge of
roofs to PR. Move R to groove and up past 78.4 to a roof. Climb
it R of 78.1A.

78.1G **Ivy Gash   HVS   (5b)
3) 85 ft./26 m. Follow a weakness R to a steep groove. Climb it
to a grassy bay and belays.

***78.2 **The Beest** E3 (5c, 5c)
1) 120 ft./36 m. Climb the steep groove to a bulge. Pull over the o/Hs (2 PR) to the R. Climb the wall to a steepening (PR) and move L to a stance. 2) 105 ft./32 m. Go R up a steep wall and move on to the scoop of 78.4. Climb pockets to the upper break on the L, move R and climb a bulge and still awkward rock to finish at the trees.

** **V Patience** HVS (5a, 4a, 5a, 4c)
1) 60 ft./18 m. As 78.2 to the bulge. TR L and move up to a ledge PB. 2) 45 ft./14 m. Go up vegetated rock to a ledge. Thread belay. 3) 45 ft./14 m. Climb the wall (2 sling runners) to the cave. 4) 70 ft./21 m. Move L, climb a crack (PR) and exit L from the grassy bay.

78.3 **West Wall Climb VS (3c, 4b, 4c, 4c)
1) 50 ft./15 m. Go L and back R through trees and up a gardened path to a tree. 2) 50 ft./15 m. Follow a curving flake, step L and up grassy rock to a tree. PB on R. 3) 50 ft./15 m. Climb up 15 ft./4 m. and TR R on to the wall. Climb direct, past a steep bulge, to the cave (PB). 4) Move L, climb a crack (PR) and exit L from the grassy bay.

***78.4 **The Eliminate** HVS (4a, 5a, 5a)
1) 90 ft./27 m. From the grass ledges, gain a diagonal fault, pass a tree and TR grass to the cave. 2) 75 ft./23 m. Move down R and TR to a groove (PR). Move R and up the rib to a stance in the rake. 2) 90 ft./27 m. Move down and R. With 1 PR, reach easier rock and climb across to a steeper section. TR R to a grassy bay. Belays high up.

***78.5 **Central Wall** VS (4a, 4b)
1) 60 ft./18 m. A gardened streak leads to disintegrating grass ledges. 2) 90 ft./27 m. Move up the wall 5 ft./2 m. and TR L 10 ft./3 m. Ascend direct until a pocketed slab leads L (threads). Move on to an upper slab and climb it to 78.1G (PB). Either abseil or continue up other climbs.

78.5A **Catharsis** E3 (5c)
2) 80 ft./24 m. TR R across a wall and up until a scoop. Step L and use pockets to a thread. Move L to belay.

***78.5B **Black Grub** E3 (4a, 5c)
1) 60 ft./18 m. as 78.5. 2) 80 ft./24 m. Follow 78.5 for a few feet, then move up R to the black streak (PR). Follow the streak (PR) to a hole and move R or go direct to finish.

78.5C **Cleo's Mood** E4 (6a)
2) 80 ft./24 m. Climb 78.5 to 15 ft./4 m. before 78.6B. Move R and climb the wall to a hole. Pull out of it and climb direct (thread on L) to a hard move. Step L to finish on 78.6A.

*78.6 **The Fly** E3 (6a)
140 ft./43 m. From the belay of 78.5, reached from the R, go into a groove on the R and climb it (PRs) to join final section of 78.1G.

78.6A **The Webb** HVS (5a)
130 ft./40 m. Go up 78.6 till it steepens. Move R on a ramp (PR) and go R up a crack and finally grass.

78.6B **The Spider** HVS (5a)
130 ft./40 m. Go up 78.6 30 ft./9 m. TR R on a smooth wall to a diagonal line. Descend to another ramp. TR to a groove and climb this, moving L to finish.

78.6C **Solution Pollution** E1 (5b)
125 ft./38 m. Start 15 ft./4 m. L of 78.7, near bush. Climb L side of a hole over bulge to holds. Climb white wall and move R to 78.6B.

78.6D **Majolica E3 (5c)
45 ft./14 m. Climb shallow groove R of 78.6C to thread. Step L and move up to hole. Move up again to wall (threads) and reach 78.6B.

***78.6E **Faience** E4 (6a)
65 ft./20 m. Climb a wall and edge on R to PR. Take a very steep wall (threads) to 78.6B. Continue direct past another thread.

78.7 **Bertram's Chimney** VD (3a, 3a)
1) 65 ft./20 m. Climb the chimney to a chockstone stance.
2) 65 ft./20 m. TR R with a difficult finish before easier ground.

78.8 **Skylight Flake**   S   (4a)

The climb is reached via a cave just R of 78.7. Go through it – the Skylight – to a ledge.   1) 80 ft./24 m. Move up to the flake and TR the slab, ascending a slight bulge to a stance and exit L to finish.

78.9 **Throwley Ridge Grooves**   S   (4a, 4a, 2c)

The large ridge separated from the main crag by a deep tree-filled gully.   1) 60 ft./18 m. Ascend steep rock on the L flank of the ridge until a move R to the groove. Go up to a stance.
2) 40 ft./12 m. Move L into the groove and climb it to the ridge.
3) 200 ft./61 m. Easy scrambling.

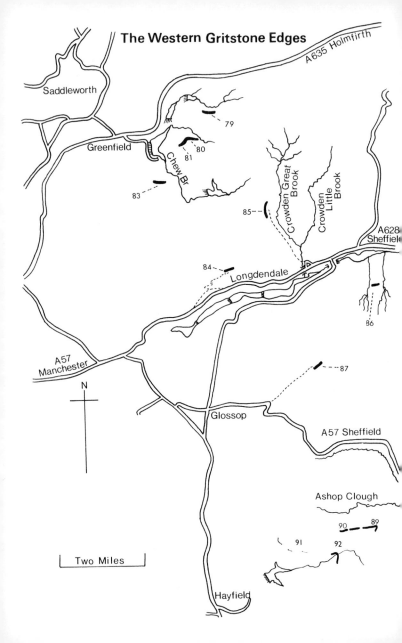

The Western Gritstone Edges

A635 Holmfirth

Saddleworth

Greenfield

Chew Br

Crowden Great Brook

Crowden Little Brook

A628 Sheffield

Longdendale

A57 Manchester

N

Glossop

A57 Sheffield

Ashop Clough

Two Miles

Hayfield

The Western Gritstone Edges

Unlike their eastern counterparts, the western edges of the Peak are neither regular nor continuous. They are scattered, immensely varied in situation and composed of natural and quarried gritstone of very variable consistency. From the stark outcrops of the Greenfield area overlooking the conurbation-jammed valleys of south Lancashire and north-east Cheshire, there is a sharp transition to the bouldery gritstone of the Bleaklow and Kinder plateaux, soft, flaky and sometimes unreliable. South of the small outcrops of the Whaley Bridge area are the bold promonotories of the Roches, large crags composed of rosy-tinted rough gritstone, while finally, beyond the boundaries of the Peak, are the isolated outcroppings of east Cheshire and north Staffordshire, quarried rock of a near basaltic smoothness at Bosley Cloud and Mow Cop, giving way to sandstones in the Churnet valley.

The intensity of climbing in these areas is likewise variable. The Roches area is the only really popular climbing ground, while there is less activity in Chew valley or Longdendale. Overall, the cliffs in this section are neglected – perhaps they will eventually channel off some of the pressure which has grown excessive on popular cliffs, like Stanage. It is not the quality of climbing which prevents development, but current fashion and dislike of walking on the part of the average modern rock climber. Ironically, these were once the most popular cliffs in the Peak.

Access

The Greenfield area cliffs are all reached from the Greenfield valley, within about one hour's walk. In Longdendale, public transport is sparse and most climbs cannot be reached from the road in less than 20–30 minutes. Most Kinder climbs take 30 minutes to one hour from the road. The small outcrops of Castel Naze and Windgather are roadside cliffs, as is the Roches. The other north Staffordshire cliffs are also quickly reached with private transport, but quite inaccessible otherwise.

Camping/accommodation

The Water Board and other owners disapprove of camping – bivouac in the Chew valley area, and in Woodhead. There is a YH at Crowden in Woodhead, suitable for reaching

Longdendale climbs and a cave at Laddow. The Barnsley MC
have a hut on the Snake and there are numerous bivouac sites
on Kinder's north edge and in the Downfall area. There is a
YH in the Edale. Camping is allowed at some of the farms near
to the Roches, and there are bivouacs, but the owner does not
approve. BMC Club or individual members are allowed by a
special agreement to camp in small groups high on Kinder and
Bleaklow, despite occasional notices to the contrary, and
always excepting the grouse massacre season.

The Chew Valley Cliffs

All the cliffs described are best approached from the George
and Dragon Hotel, Greenfield (or a point a little nearer by road
with private transport, near the reservoir yacht club).

Ravenstones   (OS Ref 035048)

An isolated bleak and black outcrop which nevertheless yields
some good climbs. It is reached in one hour's walk from below
the reservoirs above Greenfield, or in 30 minutes via Standing
Stones from the A635, and faces north so that the rock dries
slowly.

79.1A **Eastern Slab**   40 ft./12 m.   D   (2b)
Climb R of the slab centre to easier ground.

79.1   **Green Wall**   35 ft./11 m.   S   (4a)
Climb the buttress in its centre, with a mantelshelf.

79.2   **Nil Desperandum**   30 ft./9 m.   VD   (3b)
Ascend the sharp crack direct.

79.3   **Pulpit Ridge**   50 ft./15 m.   VS   (4c)
A thin crack leads to a ledge. Move L and climb the smooth
ridge.

79.3A **Guerrilla Action**   50 ft./15 m.   E2   (5b)
Go up R from the crack to the arête and continue to a ledge.

79.3B **Welcome to Greenfield**   50 ft./15 m.   E3   (5c)
Climb a wall R of 79.3A to a large break and make a hard move
on to the upper wall.

79   Ravenstones, Chew Valley

79.4 **Unfinished Arête**   60 ft./18 m.   VS   (4c)
Start on the R and go up on to the ridge, then climb it direct, escaping R below the top by a stomach-TR.

79.5 **Undun Crack**   45 ft./14 m.   VS   (4c)
Climb the crack direct.

79.6 **Slime Crack**   30 ft./9 m.
A dirty corner leads to a platform on the R. Exit on the L.

79.7 **Waterloo Climb**   40 ft./12 m.   S   (4a)
The slab L of the crack leads to platform. Stomach-TR R and climb a narrow crack.

79.8 **Mark I**   50 ft./15 m.   VD   (3a)
Climb the slab to a ledge and climb a hard crack.

79.9 **Mark II**   50 ft./15 m.   VD   (3a)
An easy chimney leads to a steepening – climb it outside.

** 79.10 **Wedgewood Crack**   70 ft./21 m.   VS   (4c)
A semi-hand-TR leads to the ridge on the L. Go up to the platform and climb the crack. A direct start is possible from the gully.

*** 79.10A **True Grit**   60 ft./18 m.   E2   (5c)
Climb the arête R of 79.10, reaching it from the gully wall.

79.10B **Sniffer Dog**   50 ft./15 m.   E1   (5b)
Climb the wall to a crack in the upper section.

79.11 **Vanishing Chimney**   25 ft./8 m.   D   (2a)
Climb the chimney high in the gully.

79.12 **Trinnacle Chimney**   30 ft./9 m.   M   (1c)
Back and foot the chimney between 79.14 and 79.15.

79.13 **Trinnacle East**   40 ft./12 m.   VS   (4c)
From the gully move R to a corner and climb it direct.

79.14 **Left Monolith**　30 ft./9 m.　S　(3c)
Straight up the L face, keeping L to finish.

79.15 **Right Monolith**　25 ft./8 m.　VS　(4c)
Climb the face direct.

79.16 **Wall and Crack**　40 ft./12 m.　S　(3c)
Easy climbing leads to a ledge. Move up with difficulty and climb a crack to the top.

79.17 **Impending Crack**　40 ft./12 m.　S　(3a)
Climb the crack, undercut to start and steep to finish.

79.18 **Subtending Wall**　40 ft./12 m.　VD　(3a)
Leave 79.17 by a sloping shelf on the R and climb the wall direct.

Dovestones Edge　(OS Ref 025040)
This gritstone edge is quite extensive, with some good climbs in its central area. It overlooks the Dovestones Reservoir in an exposed, north-west-facing position and is reached in about half an hour from Greenfield, George and Dragon.
(Photograph has not been provided for this cliff.) Climbs are described from L to R.

80.1 **The Pinnacle Route 1**　60 ft./18 m.　S　(3c)
Tr L to the arête and climb it to a ledge below the summit. Make a hard move to finish.

80.2 **Slab and Saddle**　50 ft./15 m.　VD　(3a)
Steep slabs on the L lead to a TR R to the nose.

80.3 **Wrinkled Buttress**　60 ft./18 m.　VD　(3a)
Climb the buttress by its centre, finishing by a slab.

80.4 **Curving Crack**　35 ft./11 m.　VD　(3a)
Up the slab until it curves R. Make a hard last move.

80.5 **Eyebrow**　60 ft./18 m.　S　(4a)
Tr L to a crack and ascend to a TR R to a narrow ledge. Move on to the arête to finish.

80.6 **Nasal Buttress**   50 ft./15 m.   S   (4a)
Follow the arête on the L to a ledge. Move L over the nose and finish up a steep rib.

80.7 **Central Tower**   60 ft./18 m.   VD   (3a)
Climb the buttress front direct.

80.8 **Peat Climb**   45 ft./14 m.   D   (2b)
Up a slab and chimney.

80.9 **Swan Crack**   40 ft./12 m.   VD   (3a)
Start on the arête, move R and climb the polished crack.

80.10 **Rib and Wall**   50 ft./15 m.   S   (3c)
Follow an obvious groove L of the slab to a ledge. Move R and go up the middle of the wall.

80.11 **Ferdie's Folly**   50 ft./15 m.   VS   (4c)
Pull over the bulge and continue as 80.10.

80.12 **K Climb**   50 ft./15 m.   S   (4a)
Climb the steep crack and narrow buttress.

80.13 **Kaytoo**   50 ft./15 m.   VS   (4c)
From a block, step L on to the wall, and go up small holds to a crack and big ledge. Climb the scoop on the L and step R above the overhanging corner.

80.14 **June Climb**   45 ft./14 m.   D   (2a)
Obvious cracks lead to a ledge. Go L, pull over a flake and TR across the slab to another ledge.

80.15 **Layback Crack**   35 ft./11 m.   S   (4a)
Climb the wall to a break. Step R and climb the crack.

80.16 **Tower Ridge**   85 ft./26 m.   VD   (3a)
Climb the ridge over blocks, past a crack and up walls and grass and broken rock to a final flake.

80.17 **Long Ridge**   75 ft./23 m.   VD   (3a)
From a sandy corner, exit R. Go up a chimney on the L. Scramble to a nose and final nose above.

*80.*17A **Hymen the Tactless**   50 ft./15 m.   E5   (6c)
Start on L and move up to break. Hand-TR R to wide point of
the roof, pull over and finish direct.

*80.*18 **Hanging Crack**   50 ft./15 m.   E2   (5c)
From a platform, jam the roof free.

Dovestones Quarries   (OS Ref 025040)
The great forbidding bays of the quarries are sharply in
contrast to the fairly solid, blocky, natural grit edges
hereabouts. The quarries are all large. There is loose rock, grit
and much lichen after bad weather and considerable
seriousness in the climbing. However, this seems less
exceptional now than when the climbs were first discovered in
the 1950s.

The Main Quarry

*81.*1 **Epitaph Corner**   VS   (4a, 4c)
1) 60 ft./18 m. A crack and broken rocks to a large
stance.   2) 60 ft./18 m. Climb the shallow corner on the L to a
ledge. Continue with greter difficulty to a stance.
3) 30 ft./9 m. Escape by easy ledges.

81.2 Waterfall Climb   VD   (2a, 3a, 3a, 3a)
1) 45 ft./14 m. Broken rock leads up the corner past large
blocks.   2) 35 ft./11 m. Ascend to a deep chimney by a TR.
3) 30 ft./9 m. Climb steep cracks R of the chimney.
4) 20 ft./6 m. A short wall.

*81.*3 **Garn**   HVS   (2c, 4b, 5a)
1) 55 ft./17 m. Go up R of 81.2 to a ledge.   2) 55 ft./17 m.
Climb a choked chimney in the R wall to a ledge and a shallow
corner to a ledge PB.   3) 70 ft./21 m. Climb the corner on the
L, use jams and make delicate moves to reach a crack on the R
and climb it direct.

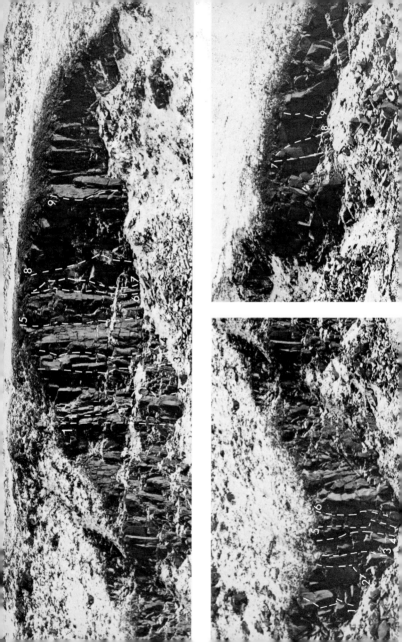

*81.4 **Mike's Meander** VS (4c, 4c, 4b)
1) 45 ft./14 m. Up a corner. 2) 70 ft./21 m. Ascend the groove to a ledge and continue by a sloping crack to a ledge. 3) 50 ft./15 m. Step R to a groove and into an exit crack.

81.5 **Initiation Groove** VS (4c, 4c)
1) 50 ft./15 m. Climb the corner to a small ledge.
2) 115 ft./35 m. The corner leads to a small ledge and final less difficult corner.

*81.6 **Brown Route** VS (4b, 4c, 4b)
1) 50 ft./15 m. Little grooves and grass lead to the groove.
2) 65 ft./20 m. Layback and jam the corner to a ledge.
3) 40 ft./12 m. A chimney leads to a final corner.

81.7 **Flutterbye Grooves** HVS (3a, 5a, 4c, 5a)
1) 35 ft./11 m. Climb a corner and go L to below an o/H.
2) 55 ft./17 m. Up to the o/H. Move R into a groove and climb to a slab. 3) 35 ft./11 m. Climb the crack past an o/H (PB).
4) 45 ft./14 m. Move L and mantelshelf into a corner and move into a final chimney. A direct finish is E1 (5b).

81.8 **White Slab HVS (3c, 5a, 5a)
1) 70 ft./21 m. Easy rocks lead to a bay. Move L to a large ledge. 2) 60 ft./18 m. Move R on to the slab (grit). Climb a groove and o/H and a block-filled crack to a ledge.
3) 40 ft./12 m. Climb steeply into cracks, with an awkward move out of the cave. These excellent climbs have suffered a major rockfall.

81.9 **Little Unicorn** VS (4c, 4c)
1) 70 ft./21 m. Climb 81.10 until a crack on the L leads to an o/H. Use 1 PA to reach a groove on the arête. Follow it to a ledge. 2) 40 ft./12 m. Step R and climb the arête.

81.10 **Titan's Groove** S (4a, 4a)
1) 60 ft./18 m. Climb the groove to a ledge (loose).
2) 30 ft./9 m. Pull over the bulge and climb the chimney.

81   opposite above: *Dovestones Main Quarry*
82   opposite below: *Dovestones Lower Quarries, Chew Valley*

The Lower Dovestones Quarries
The Left Quarry

**82.1A Tweedledum   45 ft./14 m.   (E2, 5c)

Climb easy rocks and a slab to below a groove. Climb it.

82.1 Birthday Layback   85 ft./26 m.   S   (4a)

Mantelshelf on to a shelf and climb a crack and flake, going R. Tʀ ʟ in to the corner and layback for 15 ft./4 m. Move ʀ and climb the crack.

82.2 White Wall R   75 ft./23 m.   VS   (4c)

Tʀ a shelf to the corner. Climb it to a ledge and finish up the ʟ wall.

82.3 Alumina Crack   S   (4a, 4a)

1) 40 ft./12 m. From a recess, layback a crack.   2) 60 ft./18 m. Pull over an o/ʜ to a stance and finish up the slab, keeping ʟ.

82.4 Mottled Groove   S   (4a, 3a)

1) 50 ft./15 m. The ʟ side of an arête is climbed and left by a move ʀ to a flake. Go up to a good ledge.   2) 40 ft./12 m. Climb the blocks and groove above.

82.5 Cave and Traverse   VS   (3c, 4c, 4c)

1) 30 ft./9 m. Up a slab.   2) 50 ft./15 m. Tʀ a bulge to the ʟ in to a corner. Hand-Tʀ to a second corner. Climb the groove, moving ʀ to a cave.   3) 20 ft./6 m. Enter the groove on the ʀ and ascend past loose chocks.

82.6 Blanco   S   (4a, 3c)

1) 75 ft./23 m. Climb the slab centre crack to a pedestal (ᴘʀ). Step on to the flake and pull round the o/ʜ to a ledge (ᴘʙ).
2) 40 ft./12 m. Climb slabs on the ʟ.

The Right Quarry

82.7 Ace of Spades   50 ft./15 m.   (VS, 4c)

Climb the crack to a shattered ledge and climb a corner above.

82.8 **Tiny Tim**   60 ft./18 m.   VS   (4c)
A slab leads to a horizontal break. Follow this and flakes L to the top.

***82.8A* **Bob Hope**   50 ft./15 m.   E4   (6a)
Free climb the old aid route R of 82.8.

82.9 **Pedestal Corner**   40 ft./12 m.   S   (4a)
Climb the crack (PR at top) and corner, escaping R at the top.

Wimberry Rocks   (OS Ref 016024)
By far the finest natural edge in the Chew valley area, this steep, uncompromising and north-facing cliff is particularly suitable for expert parties. There are relatively few easy climbs on it, and they are usually confined to cracks or chimneys. The cliff can be reached in half an hour from the George and Dragon, and slightly less from the road.

83.1 **Ornithologist's Corner**   40 ft./12 m.   VS   (4c)
Move up to the O/H and exit R by hard jamming.

83.2 **Surprise**   30 ft./9 m.   VS   (4c)
Climb to the nose with increasing difficulty and a final hard move over its L side.

83.3 **Overhang Chimney**   35 ft./11 m.   VS   (4c)
Climb the chimney, escaping R or L.

****83.4* **Freddie's Finale**   45 ft./14 m.   HVS   (5b)
After an initial O/H, wedge and fist jam the ferocious upper crack.

83.5 **Hanging Groove**   50 ft./15 m.   VS   (4c)
Climb the groove awkwardly and pass chocks to a groove. Continue up a crack. Other finishes exit L or R. An exit from the chock is:

V Space Shuffle   40 ft./12 m.   E4   (6a)
Hand-TR L above roof to arête. Go L to centre of O/H and L to arête, finish by groove on L.

83.6   **Coffin Crack**   50 ft./15 m.   VS   (4c)
A strenuous wide crack, especially above the niche.

***83*.7   **Trident**   70 ft./21 m.   HVS   (5a)
Climb the steep groove crack by jamming and back and foot,
escaping the Trident on the R.

83.8   **Bertie's Bugbear**   55 ft./17 m.   S   (4a)
A block is taken on the R to a scoop and crack. Exit R round the
block.

83.9   **Blue Lights Crack**   50 ft./15 m.   HVS   (5a)
Move on to the platform. Step into the crack and layback or
jam to an awkward wedging finish.

83.10   **Starvation Chimney**   50 ft./15 m.   VD   (3a)
A short crack leads to the cave. A deep crack on the R is
climbed with a narrow exit being the block. Possible! Several
other, much harder, exits are possible too!

83*.11   **Route I   50 ft./15 m.   S   (4a)
Easy cracks lead to a pulpit. Jam/layback the crack.

83*.12   **Route II   50 ft./15 m.   VS   (4c)
A thin crack and small holds lead to the pulpit. Go out R and
enter a vertical crack delicately. Finish up this.

83*.13   **Bilberry Pie   40 ft./12 m.   E4   (5c)
Climb the arête R of the chimney beyond 83.12. *Hardest* to start.

Longdendale

Though the scenery is dominated by giant reservoirs, major
roads and the remnants of the Manchester-Sheffield railway,
the valley has a charm of its own. The cliffs are found between
Tintwistle and Crowden on both the north and south sides of
the valley and are most easily reached by using private
transport. Refreshments are sometimes available at Crowden
YH, which may also be used as a convenient base.

83   Wimberry Rocks, Chew Valley

Tintwistle Knarr Quarry   (OS Ref 045993)

A compact cliff overlooking the great reservoirs a mile east of
Tintwistle. Access is forbidden and the high-standard climbs
are rarely ascended. The finest climbs are in the Central Bay.

84.1   **Levi**   60 ft./18 m.   HVS   (5a)
Climb diagonally L to a hold L of the slab. Move R and climb
the slab on small holds.

84.2   **Leprechaun**   60 ft./18 m.   VS   (4c)
Climb the corner direct, with loose rock at the top.

84.3   **Scimitar**   75 ft./23 m.   HVS   (5a)
A crack leads to a grass ledge. A curving crack joins the top of
the next climb.

84.4   **Poteen**   75 ft./23 m.   HVS   (5a)
The crack leads into a groove, which is climbed to the o/H.
Layback this and finish up a flake.

***84*.5   **Sinn Fein**   75 ft./23 m.   E2   (5c)
Climb the L side of the rib and move R below an overlap. Pull
over to a spike and mantelshelf, finishing up a slab. Poorly
protected.

****84*.6   **The Old Triangle**   80 ft./24 m.   HVS   (5a)
Climb the corner to below the o/H (PR). Exit L or R.

****84*.7   **The Arête**   75 ft./23 m.   E1   (5b)
A block is ascended. Move L to a crack and go up R to a ledge.
Climb the niche above and the final arête.

***84*.8   **Cornflake**   70 ft./21 m.   VS   (4c)
Layback the flake, with occasional jams, and move up final
short walls and ledges.

84.9   **Knobblekerry Corner**   70 ft./21 m.   VS   (4c)
Pull on to the bar and climb the L side of the corner for 20 ft./
6 m. Stride R and layback to a ledge. Climb a short corner and
a wall.

84   Tintwistle Knarr, Longdendale

** *84*.9A **Nosey Parker**   65 ft./20 m.   E4   (6a)
A hard crack leads to a ledge on its L. Step R and climb a flake above.

** *84*.10 **The Knarr Girdle**   E2
1) 60 ft./18 m. Climb route 84.4 to the O/H, move R to a spike on the rib (1 PA) and step down to TR to a small stance.   2) 50 ft./15 m. Move down and TR R to a ledge on 84.7 (PR). Move R to ledges (PB).   3) 45 ft./14 m. Cross the rockfall R to a grass ledge and more ledges to 84.9.   4) 30 ft./9 m. Hand-TR R on jams to the arête. Move R to cracks.   5) 80 ft./24 m. Go R on sloping ledges and move down to a TR R to clean-looking blocks. Hand-TR to a PR and continue to hand-TR to a groove. Move R to a ledge and ascend the groove.   6) 30 ft./9 m. Climb a grassy bay above.

Laddow Rocks   (OS Ref 064001)
Although this was once the most popular crag of all for Manchester climbers, attention has long since focused elsehwere, leaving this rather rambling cliff of knobby, but excellent, rock neglected and somewhat lichenous. It can be readily reached in about half an hour's walk from Crowden or a little over one hour from Greenfield by a good path. It is north-east-facing and therefore slow-drying.

85.1 **Pillar Chimney**   60 ft./18 m.   VD   (3a)
A shallow corner is left by a TR R.

85.2 **Pillar Ridge**   70 ft./21 m.   (3c)
A worn crack leads to a platform on the L. Climb a wall left of the ridge, mantelshelf up on to it and climb the buttress above.

85.3 **V Arête**   65 ft./20 m.   (3c)
An arête is reached via an awkward short wall. Climb on the R of the arête to a stance (PB). Step up R and move on to the arête to finish.

84.7   *Keith Sharples on The Arête, Tintwistle Knarr*

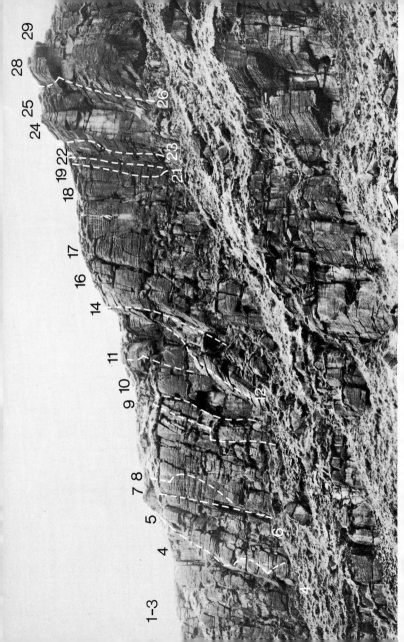

85.4 **Cyclops' Wall**   60 ft./18 m.   VS   (4c)
The buttress is climbed on the L, using a crack to a gully ledge.
Climb the buttress, overcoming an O/H.

85.5 **Siren's Rock**   75 ft./23 m.   S   (4a)
Climb the buttress on the R to a ledge. Move up L to a crack.
Move on to the ridge and finish using a hold on the R.

85.6 **Scylla**   60 ft./18 m.   D   (2a)
A chimney L of the ridge leads to a roof. Exit L to easy rock and
a final chimney.

85.7 **Priscilla Ridge   65 ft./18 m.   HVS   (5a)
Ascend the lower buttress. Go straight up via an overhanging
crack to the obvious ridge and follow it up. (Thread under top
section.)

85.8 **Priscilla   75 ft./23 m.   VS   (4c)
Go up the lower buttress. Take the ridge on the L and go
diagonally R to a shallow groove and block belay. Go back L by
a higher-level TR and finish up the centre of the upper wall.

85.9 **Terrace Chimney**   70 ft./21 m.   VD   (3a)
Go up L of the obvious crack, deviating L.

85.10 **Terrace Crack**   50 ft./15 m.   S   (3c)
Climb the crack direct.

85.11 **Terrace Wall**   VS   (4c, 4c)
1) 35 ft./11 m. From the flake, go up to a ledge. Go L and up to
a ledge via a corner. Move L and ascend a depression to a
ledge.   2) 25 ft./8 m. Step on to a block on the L. Move R on to
the corner and ascend.

***85.12 **Long Climb**   VD   (3c, 3c)
1) 55 ft./17 m. Climb the centre of the worn slab, with a slight
deviation R.   2) 55 ft./17 m. Climb a scoop and cracks to a
corner, finishing up a crack.

85.13 **Leaf Buttress**   55 ft./17 m.   VS   (4c)
Climb the little buttress by a corner on the L and move R on to the front. Go up the leaf flake and climb the bulge above.

85.14 **Leaf Crack**   55 ft./17 m.   S   (4a)
From a platform above blocks, climb the crack to a ledge R of the Leaf. Pull round the o/H and a scratched wall above.

85.15 **Little Crowberry**   65 ft./20 m.   S   (3c)
Tr L from the bottom of the ridge, swing L on to the wall and ascend to the Pulpit. Move up to two cracks and TR L to a scoop. Go up a shallow crack to a good ledge.

***85*.16 **Long Chimney Ridge**   65 ft./20 m.   VD   (3a)
Pull on to the ridge and follow it to a ledge. Move up to vertical cracks (as 85.15), and climb them and a buttress above.

85.17 **Long Chimney**   50 ft./15 m.   D   (2c)
Follow the chimney throughout.

85.18 **Straight Chimney**   60 ft./18 m.   M   (1b)
Climb to a ledge and go up the chimney above.

85.19 **Garden Wall**   60 ft./18 m.   VD   (3a)
Move up the wall L of the chimney and step R to the chimney. Move into a right-angled corner and climb it direct.

85.20 **Left Twin Chimney**   60 ft./18 m.   M   (1c)
Climb the chimney direct.

85.21 **Twin Eliminate**   50 ft./15 m.   HVS   (5a)
Go up the buttress to twin thin cracks. Climb the cracks to a mantelshelf (hard) and go up to a ledge. Go up to the o/H on the L and swing over the nose to easier climbing.

85.22 **Right Twin Chimney**   50 ft./15 m.   VD   (3a)
The chimney is climbed awkwardly.

****85*.23 **Tower Face**   55 ft./17 m.   VS   (4b)
Pull over the undercut and go up to a ledge. Take the scoop and TR to a ledge on the R. From the L edge of the ledge, go up the crack, or the face to the L (4c).

85.24 **Tower Arête**   55 ft./17 m.   VS   (4c)
Ascend a block and the arête to the ledge. Continue more easily.

85.25 **North Climb**   60 ft./18 m.   D   (2c)
A large slab is climbed to a crack on the L edge of 85.26. Make a delicate TR to a crack on the L. Finish up this.

85.26 **North Wall**   55 ft./17 m.   S   (4a)
The wall is climbed on the R to a ledge. Climb the O/H.

*85.27 **Cave Arête Indirect**   60 ft./18 m.   VS   (4c)
Pull on to the stance and swing on to the arête. Continue to a ledge. Pull over the bulge, with a hard move to easier rock.

85.28 **Cave Arête   55 ft./17 m.   S   (4a)
A scoop on the L of the cave is climbed to a delicate TR R to the arête. Climb to the ledge. From the block, hand-TR L to the edge and finish direct.

85.29 **Cave Crack   50 ft./15 m.   VS   (4c)
Pull out of the cave and climb to the ledge. Finish as 85.28.

Shining Clough   (OS Ref 098986)
North-facing and rather grim of aspect, situated well above the 1,600 ft./500 m. contour, Shining Clough is nevertheless a very pleasant cliff on closer aquaintance and in dry conditions. It gives a variety of climbs, several of them of the highest quality, and yet seems to be relatively unfrequented. It can be reached in about 30 minutes from the B6105 near Crowden, by a stiff uphill walk.

86.1 **Electra**   55 ft./17 m.   HVS   (5a)
A wide crack is climbed to a ledge. Continue direct.

86.2 **Orestes   45 ft./14 m.   E2   (5c)
From a ledge, move L to a groove and climb it, exiting L. Move up to a sling on the R. Make a long final reach. The thin crack on the L gives Chalkman (E2, 5c).

86.3 **Oedipus**   60 ft./18 m.   VS   (4c)
Climb the crack and move R to the corner.

86.4 **Birthday Corner**   55 ft./17 m.   VS   (4c)
Jam and layback the corner crack.

86.5 **Monkey Puzzle**   35 ft./11 m.   S   (4a)
Go up the wide crack, TR R and go up a second wide crack.

*86.6 **East Rib**   40 ft./12 m.   E1   (5c)
Move R to the arête and climb the crack and arête. Serious.
Direct it is even more so (E3, 6a). The right wall gives Icon
(HVS, 5a).

86.7 **East Chimney**   60 ft./18 m.   M   (1c)
Climb the chimney, exiting behind chocks.

***86.8 **Atherton Brothers**   70 ft./21 m.   S   (4a)
A flake crack is climbed to a wall, which leads into a chimney
on the R. Exit outside the chockstones.

***86.9 **Phoenix**   85 ft./26 m.   VS   (4c)
Take the crack, moving L to a stance. Climb the corner crack to
the arête and go up to the top.

***86.10 **Via Principia**   80 ft./24 m.   S   (4a)
Climb a crack on the R to a ledge. Go L to the arête, up and
back R by a steep crack and wall. You can escape the ledge by a
chimney to the R (3a) or by a layback flake to its R (4c).

***86.11 **Birthday Chimney**   80 ft./24 m.   VD   (3a)
Climb the chimney. Above and R are Short Crack (VS, 4c),
Satyr on the Central Buttress (E2, 5b) and Solstice on the
R-hand buttress (HVS, 5a).

*86.11A **Some Product**   35 ft./11 m.   E1   (5b)
Climb the flake L of 86.12 on its L wall, taking a scoop *en route*.

86.11B **Saucius Digitalis**   35 ft./11 m.   E3   (6a)

Ascend the L wall of 86.12 by a thin crack. Above it move L then R.

86.12 **Nagger's Delight**   35 ft./11 m.   HVS   (5a)

Ascend the steep corner to a hard (dirty) finish.

86.13 **Naaden**   35 ft./11 m.   HVS   (5a)

Climb the crack on the wall, with a thin move where it ends.

86.14 **Yerth**   45 ft./14 m.   E2   (5c)

Pull over an o/H and reach a crack which leads to a block. Move up and round to the R and mantelshelf fiercely on to a ledge. Easier above.

86.15 **Pisa**   55 ft./17 m.   VS   (4c)

The wall L of the arête is climbed by cracks which end. Move up and R to a ledge. Pull over the o/H above.

86.16 **Galileo**   60 ft./18 m.   E1   (5b)

A thin crack leads to a large ledge. Follow a second crack to Pisa ledge. Finish as 86.15.

86.17 **Pisa Direct**   75 ft./23 m.   VS   (4c)

Climb the arête to a ledge and smooth crack. Go up to the detached block, TR L 15 ft./4 m. and reach a ledge. Attain the Pisa ledge. Finish as 86.15.

86.18 **Pisa Super Direct**   65 ft./20 m.   VS   (5a)

As 86.17 to the detached block. Take the cracks above direct with difficulty.

86.19 **Stable Cracks**   55 ft./17 m.   S   (4a)

Climb a steep crack, awkward in places, to the top.

86.20 **Typist's Chimney**   55 ft./17 m.   D   (2b)

The chimney leads to a ledge and second chimney.

86.23   Keith Sharples on Big Wall, Shining Clough

86.21 **Unicorn Cracks** 55 ft./17 m. S (4a)

A sloping crack on the R leads to a scoop, exit R and climb to a ledge. Finish up the corner.

86.22 **Trungel Crack** 60 ft./18 m. HVS (5a)

Go up to the sentry box and leave it, with difficulty, for a ledge on the R. Climb the crack above and the crack L of the corner of 86.21.

86.23 **Big Wall** 65 ft./20 m. E2 (5c)

Take the crack to an O/H, move L and reach a small ledge. Climb the crack until a move L to a ledge. Reach a cave and continue direct.

86.24 **Gremlin Groove 50 ft./15 m. VS (4c)

Climb a crack to a ledge and climb the groove past a bulge to an easier groove. Just L is Holme Moss (HVS, 5b).

86.25 **Toadstool Crack** 35 ft./11 m. VD (3b)

Climb the crack through O/HS.

86.26 **Pinnacle Crack** 40 ft./12 m. S (4a)

A crack is jammed until a TR R is possible to a ledge. Climb the crack L to the arête and move R on to the nose.

86.27 **Pinnacle Face** 30 ft./9 m. VS (4c)

Climb the centre of the face and move L to the arête. From a ledge, a bulge is climbed to the top.

86.28 **Ordinary Route** 15 ft./4 m. M (1c)

Large holds lead up the back of the Pinnacle.

Kinder North Edge (OS Ref 099891)

This very extensive area of cliffs faces north, overlooking the Snake (A57) road. It can be reached in about 40 minutes from the road. The cliffs are remote, slow-drying and often gritty with some loose rock, and almost never climbed despite excellent routes. The lichenous rough rock gives many extremely fierce jamming problems.

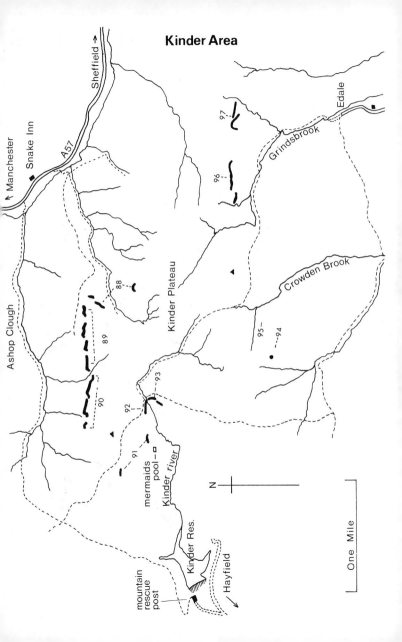

Kinder Area

Sheffield →
← Manchester
Snake Inn
A57
Ashop Clough
Edale
Grindsbrook
97
96
Kinder Plateau
Crowden Brook
88
89
90
95
94
92
93
91
mermaids pool
Kinder river
N
Kinder Res.
Hayfield →
mountain rescue post
One Mile

Chinese Wall   (OS Ref 099891)

87.1 **Passe**   50 ft./15 m.   VS   (4c)
A wall L of a groove leads to the terrace. Finish by a wide
fist-jamming crack.

87.2 **Malaise**   50 ft./15 m.   VS   (4c)
Go up the groove and a flake to the terrace. Move R and finish
by a thin crack.

87.3 **Corner Crack**   40 ft./12 m.   S   (3c)
The corner crack has an awkward exit.

*87.4 **Tryphon**   45 ft./14 m.   VS   (4c)
A thin crack leads on to the slab. Move up R, finishing on the R
arête.

87.5 **Necrosis   50 ft./15 m.   S   (3c)
Climb the crack L of the cave, exit R and mantelshelf on upper
wall.

Fairbrook Buttress   (OS Ref 096896)

***88.1 **Misty Wall**   60 ft./18 m.   S   (4a)
A face L of the arête is climbed to an O/H. Pull over to easier
ground above. To the L is Round Up (HVS, 5b) and R, Wind
Wall (HVS, 5a). Its direct is E2 (5c).

88.2 **Trojan**   35 ft./11 m.   HVS   (5b)
Pull into a niche and overcome the O/H from a hanging block
with difficulty. The L-hand face is Cassandra (E2, 5b).

87   opposite above: *Chinese Wall*
88   opposite below: *Fairbrook Buttress, Kinder*

Ashop Edge (OS Ref 095898)

Cabin Buttress

89.1 **Hanging Chimney**   45 ft./14 m.   VS   (3a)
The chimney is climbed direct with a hard finish.

89.1A **Pneumoconiosis**   40 ft./12 m.   VS   (4c)
Climb the wall R of 89.1 to a short crack and round finish.

89.1B **Brains Missing**   45 ft./14 m.   E2   (5b)
From the R end of the wall, climb to a short crack 6 ft./2 m. R of it. Climb this.

89.2 **Hanging Chimney Wall**   45 ft./14 m.   S   (3c)
A wall leads to a ledge (30 ft./9 m.). Go R and finish up a chimney.

89.3 **Cavern Climb**   60 ft./18 m.   VD   (3a)
A corner leads to a boulder-cave. Go through a hole on the R to a ledge. Climb the crack on the L.

89.4 **Jactation**   65 ft./20 m.   VS   (4c)
Quit a pedestal and ascend the central wall to a cave. Go L up a crack to the roof, move L past a flake to the arête. Go up to the o/h and up a final crack.

89.5 **East Chimney**   50 ft./15 m.   M   (1c)
Bridge the deep chimney and go R to a ledge. A crack leads to the top.

89.6 **Ashop Corner**   40 ft./12 m.   S   (4a)
Climb a corner crack and finish on the R. For the V, Roman – TR R along the lip of the o/h to finish up 89.7 (s).

89.7* **Ashop Crack   60 ft   VS   4c.
Go up to the ledge. Enter the crack with difficulty and continue more easily.

88.1   *Misty Wall, Fairbrook Buttress. Paul Nunn*

*89.8 Ashop Climb   60 ft   VD   3a.
Go up to the ledge. Traverse R and climb the chimney.

***89.9 Eureka   60 ft   VS   4c.
Attain a ledge under the roof. Enter the corner and traverse L under the roof, pulling onto the upper steep face.

89.10 Trial Balance   40 ft./12 m.   HVS   (5a)
Up shallow pockets, move L and ascend an overhanging crack to a ledge. Move R to short cracks and an uncompromising finish. Britt's Cleavage (E1, 5b) goes L from the ledge over the roof.

Brothers Buttress   (OS Ref 092898)

***89.11 Legacy   65 ft./20 m.   HVS   (5a)
From the buttress centre, move up and follow a crack L then back R to a vertical crack. Move R and climb the arête.

* V Intestate   HVS   (5b)
From the vertical crack, move L and climb a thin crack to sloping shelves and a final awkward crack.

*89.12 Brothers Eliminate   60 ft./18 m.   HVS   (5a)
From the buttress centre, move up to a crack and jam two O/HS to the crack above and a recess. Go L to a stance and up the wall. Big Brother (E2, 5c) takes the undercut on the L and crack above.

89.13 Little Boy Blue   60 ft./18 m.   HVS   (5b)
Move up to the bulge and wall above. TR L to the ledge. Go R to a block, TR L and finish up the buttress centre.

89.14 Dirty Trick   30 ft./9 m.
A short wall leads to a shelf on the L. Climb an overhanging corner to another shelf and final block.

89A   top: *Ashop Edge*
89B   middle: *Brothers Buttress*
89C   below: *Black Overhang, Kinder North*

89.15 **Round Chimney** 40 ft./12 m. VD (3a)
Go up the chimney direct.

89.16 **Razor Crack** 40 ft./12 m. S (4a)
The clean crack, exiting R.

89.17 **Dunsinane** 55 ft./17 m. VS (4c)
Move up to a central break. Move R to a flake and across to the arête finish. The Savage Breast (E1, 5b) starts up the wall on the R and crosses 89.17.

89.18 **Pot Belly** 50 ft./15 m. E1 (5c)
Go up to the o/H (thread). Move over and up the face with difficulty.

V Tum Tum HVS (5a)
Move R from the thread and enter a groove with difficulty. Above it is easier.

The Black Overhang (OS Ref 089898)

89.19 **Tambourine** 35 ft./11 m. D (2b)
Go up the walls R of shallow slabs and over the first large o/H. Keep R where the slabs narow.

89.20 **Scooper Dooper** 70 ft./21 m. VD (3a)
Go L along horizontal cracks almost to the edge of the o/H and up slabs to a ledge. Finish up the scooped wall.

89.21 **Backhammer** 50 ft./15 m. S (4a)
A green corner leads to a TR L on to the slab. Climb its R edge.

** 89.22 **Downbyne** 80 ft./24 m. S (4a)
Ledgy rock is climbed, moving R to ledges. Pull up R of the rib to a slab and exit L to a niche. Move L to a final rounded rib.

89.23 **Whit Walk** 60 ft./18 m. D (2a)
A shallow corner leads to a pointed rock and ledge. Go up a bulging corner direct.

89.24 **The Kinder Caper**   60 ft./18 m.   VS   (4c)
Up the slanting crack to the roof. Climb a hanging crack to a
ledge. Step up and TR L to a ledge. Move up to a better ledge
(belay). Move R to a slab over the lower cracks and finish direct
over a roof.

89.25 **Per Ardua   65 ft./20 m.   VS   (4c)
Up the smooth wall to a move R under the O/H to a ledge. Go L
over a loose block. Climb an impressive crack.

Jester Buttress   (OS Ref 083897)
To the left is:

90.1 **Exodus   60 ft./18 m.   VS   (4c)
Move out of the cave to the roof and TR L to the first corner.
Layback the O/H to another corner. Climb a second O/H to a
stance on the L. Climb the crack in the slab direct.

90.2 **Jester Cracks   50 ft./15 m.   VS   (4c)
A short slab leads to a ledge. Climb a thin crack near the arête
to a ledge. Go L and climb the final crack.

*90.3 **Lobster Crack**   45 ft./14 m.   VS   (4c)
Take the crack to the ledge and its counterpart above.

90.4 **Crab Crack**   45 ft./14 m.   HVS   (5a)
Take the two R-hand cracks with a hard start.

90.4A **Wizzard**   55 ft./17 m.   VS   (4c)
Move R from the base of 90.4 to the buttress front. Go up to a
loose block and move L to finish on the edge.

90.5 **Woe is Me**   30 ft./9 m.   VD   (3a)
A wide crack is awkward, especially at its finale.

90.6 **Broken Buttress**   60 ft./18 m.   D   (2b)
Climb three successive large blocks.

Dead Chimney Buttress   (OS Ref 079898)

90.7 **Honeymoon Route**   40 ft./12 m.   VD   (3a)
Go easily up the gully face to a ledge. A chimney above is followed. An outside finish is possible but hard.

90.8 **Parliamentary Climb**   60 ft./18 m.   VS   (4c)
Follow a fierce crack to a good ledge and a narrow crack above. The L-hand crack is vs also.

90.9 **Dead Chimney**   40 ft./12 m.   VS   (4c)
Enter the chimney with difficulty, and exit R with difficulty at the top.

Kinder Downfall Ravine

Upper Western Buttress   (OS Ref 073892)
A broken crag in a prominent position overlooking the entrance to the Kinder Downfall valley. Though broken there is some good climbing in the central area, where the looser broken section merges into short solid walls. The cliff is reached in about 35 minutes from the road below the Kinder reservoir.

91.1 **Candle Buttress**   50 ft./15 m.   VS   (4b)
Pull over the o/H and move on to the buttress. Climb it delicately.

91.2* **Extinguisher Chimney   50 ft./15 m.   VS   (4c)
Go into the depths of the chimney, move up and chimney to the edge. Pull over an awkward bulge to easier ground.

91.2A **Dark Side of the Moon**   60 ft./18 m.   E2   (5b)
Ascends the buttress L of 91.2. Climb past the thread and up the rib, move L and finish up a wall.

91.3 **Central Gully**   100 ft./30 m.   S   (3b)
An easy corner leads to ledges and a steep wall. Follow a deep cleft R of the nose. Several variations are possible.

90A   middle: *Jester Crack Area*
90B   below: *Dead Chimney Buttress, Kinder North Edge*

Kinder Buttress (OS Ref 078888)

***91.4 **Mermaid's Ridge**   S   (4a, 4a)
1) 50 ft./15 m. Ascend the ridge, past a bulge, to the terrace.   2) 50 ft./15 m. Tʀ on to the arête from the ʟ and climb a groove to finish.

91.5 **Right Twin Chimney   VS   (4a, 4a, 3c)
1) 20 ft./18 m. Climb a shallow chimney to the terrace.   2) 25 ft./8 m. A steep chimney is awkward to enter. Belay on the ʟ above.   3) 35 ft./11 m. Move ʀ and climb a chimney.

91.6 **Atone**   55 ft./17 m.   HVS   (5a)
Go up the gully wall to a steep crack. Climb it with difficulty.

Kinder Downfall – The Amphitheatre   (OS Ref 082889)
Where the River Kinder plunges over a rugged cliff, it abruptly abandons the Kinder plateau and flows down a narrow valley to the reservoir. The ravine below the Downfall has cliffs on both its flanks, perched high above subsidiary buttresses and unstable earth and loose rock. To the north is the Amphitheatre, an upper and lower semi-circle of quite sound gritstone cliffs which catch the sun and give good climbing.

92.1 **Domino Wall**   55 ft./17 m.   HVS   (5b)
Climb a friable wall and move up to an o/ʜ. Pull over it and move ʀ to a shelf. The wall above is deceptively difficult. Poorly protected.

92.2 **Raggald's Wall**   55 ft./17 m.   HVS   (5a)
An overhanging groove is climbed to a niche. Move ʟ and mantelshelf in an exposed situation.

***92.3 **Great Chimney Left Hand**   60 ft./18 m.
VS   (4c)
An overhanging groove is climbed to a niche. Make awkward moves to a ledge. Up the wall on the ʟ and a blunt arête.

91   *Upper Western Buttress, Kinder Buttress*
92   *The Amphitheatre, Kinder Down Fall Area*

***92.4 **Great Chimney**   60 ft./18 m.   S   (4a)
Move up and layback to a ledge. Move L and back R into a final chimney.

* **V Encore Exit**   50 ft./15 m.   VS   (4c)
From the ledge, move up and R. Climb the steep buttress to a sloping finish.

92.5 **Professor's Chimney   40 ft./12 m.   D   (2b)
Start in the R-hand crack and finish on the L.

92.6 **Left-Fork Chimney   55 ft./17 m.   D   (2a)
Up the chimney and L on good holds.

92.7 **Right-Fork Chimney**   60 ft./18 m.   VD   (3a)
From the fork, go R and wedge a final bulge.

92.8 **Embarkation Parade   70 ft./21 m.   VS   (4c)
A wall leads into the groove, which is followed to a ledge on the R. Exit by a short crack.

92.9 **Crooked Overhang**   65 ft./20 m.   VS   (4b)
Tr from L to R to mantelshelves, and a cave. Overcome the o/h awkwardly and finish up the chimney.

***92.10 **Zigzag Climb**   55 ft./17 m.   VD   (3a)
Go up L and take polished cracks to a stance. Move up and R to a short polished crack.

The Lower Amphitheatre

92.11 **North Tier Climb   90 ft./27 m.   VS   (4c, 4b)
Jam and layback to the terrace. Move L and climb a wall. Move R to a hole and up a short crack.

92.11A **The Glorious Twelfth**   70 ft./21 m.   E1   (5b)
Climb a groove about 35 ft./11 m. L of the arête of Dove Crag. Friable overhanging and difficult to finish.

92.11B **The Hunter**   100 ft./30 m.   E1   (5b)
Start in the middle of the wall 15 ft./4 m. L of the arête. Climb a flake, move L to a flake and go up this to a niche and finish up the wall.

92.11C **The Beast**   95 ft./29 m.   HVS   (5b)
From the same point, go up the wall to the o/ʜ and move ʀ to the cave. Climb an arête to a ledge and finishing groove.

92.11D **The Bloody Thirteenth**   75 ft./23 m.   HVS   (5a)
Enter the steep crack from the L. Climb it and the rib to the cave. Finish up a groove on the ʀ. Shotgun Groove (HVS, 5b) is the shallow groove just ʀ.

92.12 **Downfall Groove**   55 ft./17 m.   HVS   (5a)
Jam the wide and usually wet crack, with a hard move at 20 ft./6 m. A fierce climb. Thin crack just L is Poacher's Crack (HVS, 5a) and that ʀ, Independence Crack (ʜᴠꜱ, 5a, 1 sling ᴀ).

Kinder Downfall   (OS Ref 083888)

93.1 Downfall Climb   120 ft./36 m.   M   (1c)
Climb the ʀ corner of the fall. Tʀ shelves and a series of cracks to exit on the L side of the fall. Inadvisable in very wet conditions and excellent in occasional good, frozen winter conditions, when the fall can also be done direct at a fairly high standard (ice–IV).

*** **V South Corner**   60 ft./18 m.   VD   (3b)
From the bay above the first section of 93.1, enter a crack leading to a bulge. Pull over and go up a deep chimney to finish.

93.2 **Twopenny Tube**   70 ft./21 m.   D   (2b)
Ascend the innards of the chimney to an outside stance and exit above with difficulty.

Great Buttress (OS Ref 083887)

**93.3 Central Chimney 75 ft./23 m. D (2c)
Go up the deep chimney to a steepening. Exit L (stance). Climb an overhanging crack above.

V Direct VS (4c)
Go straight up the upper chimney. Often wet.

***93.4 Gomorrah 90 ft./27 m. VS 4(c)
Up easy rock to an O/H, pull over this on the L and climb a crack through bulges. Finish R of the nose.

**93.5 Sodom 75 ft./23 m. VD (3a)
Follow an easy gully and its continuation, a wide crack, to a bay. Move R to finish.

***93.6 Trio Wall 80 ft./24 m. VS (4c)
Easy rock leads to a cave. Start the wall on the L and go up and R to a niche. Move R and climb crack.

93.7 Pigeon Corner 65 ft./20 m. VS (4c)
Go up to the cave. A steep move leads into the awkward corner, which can be left on the R or climbed direct.

**93.8 Pocket Wall 65 ft./20 m. VS (4b)
Ascend easily to the ledge. A pock-marked wall is climbed, trending R, to three slabby steps in the upper reacher. Poorly protected.

***93.9 Great Slab 55 ft./17 m. S (4a)
A thin crack (sand) leads to a stance at 40 ft./12 m. (PB). Climb the steep wall.

93.1 Kinder Downfall in winter

***93.10 **Girdle Traverse**   330 ft./100 m.   VS   (4a, 4a, 4c, 4c, 4b, 4a)

A serious climb requiring general VS competence in the party.   1) 45 ft./14 m. The crack is climbed and moves R followed to the ledge. Go R to belay.   2) 60 ft./18 m. Move R across two ribs to a wall and either go straight across or mantelshelf before traversing R to a ledge which leads to 93.3.   3) 55 ft./17 m. Go R and TR under overhangs to 93.8 with difficulty. Go down to a belay.   4) 60 ft./18 m. Follow a break across to 93.9 and move into the niche. Move R and stride 93.7 to good threads.   5) 50 ft./15 m. Descend a little and TR 94.6 and below an o/H to a chimney.   6) 60 ft./18 m. Cross a ledge and rib and move down to a crack. Finish up 93.10.

Kinder Southern Edges

The cliffs overlooking Edale are more friendly, sunnier and less green than their northerly counterparts. Nevertheless, they still demand walking for at least 30 minutes and are little ascended. Some hard climbs have probably never been repeated here. The rock is quite variable, though at best it is excellent.

The Pagoda   (OS Ref 099868)

A rounded and eccentric tower, it can be reached in 30 minutes from Upper Booth, Edale, or a little over one hour from the Hayfield road end.

94.1 **Morrison's Route**   55 ft./17 m.   S   (4a)

Climb the L corner to a terrace. Finish by either the L corner of the upper wall or by its centre.

94.2 **Hartley's Route   65 ft./20 m.   HVS   (5a)

An overhanging crack leads to a ledge. Move R to a flake and up to a ledge. Follow a crack and TR R. Mantelshelf L to a ledge and exit up a bulge above the boulder.

93   Kinder Downfall Ravine and Great Buttress

***94.3 **Herford's Route**   60 ft./18 m.   S   (4a)
A scratched wall leads to a ledge, also attainable from the R.
Move L and follow rounded holds and cracks. Dewsbury's
Route (HVS, 5b) takes the R-hand start and goes direct.

Crowden Clough Face   (OS Ref 095870)

95.1 **Central Route**   55 ft./17 m.   VS   (4c)
Reach the main crack from a crack on the L. Follow the crack
past a difficult chockstone.

95.2 **Middle Chimney**   40 ft./12 m.   M   (1c)
Climb the chimney direct.

95.3 **Chimney and Sab**   45 ft./14 m.   S   (3c)
Go up 15 ft./4 m. to a ledge. Climb a slab on the L. Other exits
are possible.

Upper Tor   (OS Ref 114876)
Pleasantly situated, overlooking Grindsbrook is one of Kinder's
best cliffs, a regular steep outcrop with varied and excellent
climbing; 30 minutes from Edale.

***96.1 **Upper Tor Wall**   60 ft./18 m.   S   (4a)
Ascend a little groove and pull on to a ledge. Follow very steep
cracks and a wall to a second ledge. Move up on the R to finish.

96.2 **Hiker's Gully   60 ft./18 m.   M   (1c)
Climb the gully line with numerous variants.

96.3 **Hiker's Crack**   50 ft./15 m.   VD   (3a)
Reach the crack from the gully – it is awkward.

96.4 **Hiker's Chimney**   50 ft./15 m.   S   (4a)
Reach the chimney by a hand-tr from the gully to a point
beyond the crack. Difficulty increases below the final
chockstones.

94   above: *The Pagoda, Kinder South*
95   below: *Crowden Clough Face, Kinder South*

96.5 **The Ivory Tower**   75 ft./23 m.   HVS   (5b)
A bulge 15 ft./4 m. R of the gully leads to a ledge. Climb a crack to the o/H move R to a stance (belay). Move back L and pull over a bulge and TR to a thin crack. Climb it with difficulty, moving R. Finish up a wall.

96.6 **Artillery Chimney**   45 ft./14 m.   S   (4a)
Follow the crack to the 'gun'. Pull over it on the R and finish by a rounded bulge.

96.7 **Brutality**   45 ft./14 m.   HVS   (5a)
A corner leads to the o/H, swing R and climb to a second o/H. Hand-TR L to a groove with difficulty.

96.8 **Robert**   45 ft./14 m.   E1   (5b)
Slabs lead to the bulge, TR L to a stance. Jam the crack over the bulge.

96.9 **Pedestal Wall**   45 ft./14 m.   VD   (3a)
Go up the slabs from L to R to a groove. Move R to the pedestal and up a wall above. A L-hand exit is HVS (5a).

Nether Tor   (OS Ref 123876)
A little less friendly than Upper Tor and rather looser, Nether Tor has some excellent climbs nevertheless. A recent rock-fall has obliterated part of the central section. Thirty minutes from Edale.

97.1A **Beautiful Losers**   70 ft./21 m.   E1   (5b)
Climb a crack to a ledge. Hand-TR R 20 ft./6 m. to a flake, climb it and an o/H and make a mantelshelf move, then climb the rib, finishing L.

***97.1 **Moneylender's Crack**   60 ft./18 m.   VS   (4c)
Enter the Kestrel's Cave and overcome the o/H. Continue by awkward but good climbing.

96   *Upper Tor Grindsbrook, Kinder South*
96.1   *Upper Tor Wall, Steve Belk climbing (page 274)*
97   *Nether Tor Grindsbrook, Kinder South (page 275)*

97.1B **Mortgage Wall**   65 ft./18 m.   HVS   (5b)
Climb the crack R of 97.1 to a grass ledge, and the wall above.

97.2 **Linden Groove**   60 ft./18 m.   D   (2c)
Climb ledges and a crack to an upper wall – various finishes are available.

***97.3 **Snooker Route**   90 ft./27 m.   VS   (4c)
A pocketed wall leads to a tattered holly. Up a block to a small ledge. TR L, with awkward moves, to easier ground. Exit via a small chimney.

97.4 **Hot Flush Crack   70 ft./21 m.   HVS   (5a)
A 'boulder problem' scoop leads to the R arête and ledges under the roof (thread). Move L to a crack and climb it.

97.5 **Flash Wall   70 ft./21 m.   VS   (4c)
A rounded crack leads to the ledges (97.4) thread. Move R on to the wall and go up direct via a wide polished crack, or TR L pulling over the nose spectacularly.

97.6 **Caesar Ridge**   80 ft./24 m.   S   (3c)
Start up a little flake crack on the wall of the gully and continue up the ridge above.

97.7 **Roman Nose**   80 ft./24 m.   S   (3c)
Ascend a slab R of the cave. Mantelshelf into a corner and escape R after a few feet over the nose. Belay on a ledge above and finish up chimneys.

Castle Naze   (OS Ref 054785)
A compact, polished and uncompromising little crag with a few classic problems which have suited most tastes since about 1914. A popular cliff among beginners. Care is needed in belaying on a loose top. the first climbs are all about 30–40 ft./9–12 m.

98.1 **Nithin**   VD   (3a)
An arête leads to a shelf. Move L to a chimney.

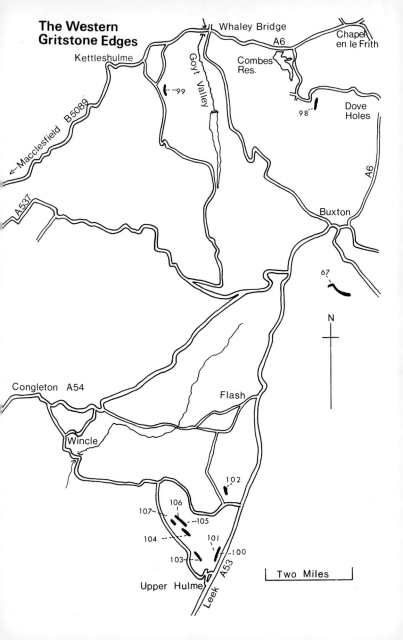

The Western
Gritstone Edges

Whaley Bridge

Kettleshulme

Combes
Res.

Chapel
en le Frith

A6

~99

Govt Valley

98~

Dove
Holes

B5089

Macclesfield

A6

A537

Buxton

67~

N

Congleton A54

Flash

Wincle

102

106

107~

~105

104 ~

101

103~

~100

Upper Hulme

Leek A53

Two Miles

98.2 **Flake Crack** S (4a)
The L wall is climbed from L to R to a shelf. Layback the crack.

*98.3 **Flywalk** VD (3a)
Follow a polished crack and the edge to the L, and exit R.

*98.4 **Niche** S (3c)
Enter the niche and exit with difficulty.

98.5 **Niche Arête** S (4a)
The delicate arête.

*98.6 **Studio** VD (3a)
Start on the L, mantelshelf slightly R and climb a crack.

98.7 **A P Chimney** VD (3a)
The corner crack is hardest at the chock.

98.8 **Pilgrim's Progress** S (4a)
A thin crack leads to the arête.

98.9 **Little Pillar** VD (3a)
A steep crack and pillar lead to a ledge. Go up L.

98.10 **No Name** VD (3a)
A crack leads to the ledge on the R. Climb the corner.

*98.11 **Keep Corner** S (3c)
An awkward corner leads to a ledge. The top is difficult also.

98.12 **Keep Arête S (4a)
Follow the arête, which is delicate, steep and poorly protected.

98.13 **Scoop Face VS (4c)
Polished shelves lead to the scoop. Tʀ R, climb the wall and exit L. Can be protected with cunning. A direct start is suitable for scoffing experts (5c).

98.14 **Footstool** D (2a)
The break R of Keep Buttress.

98   Castle Naze

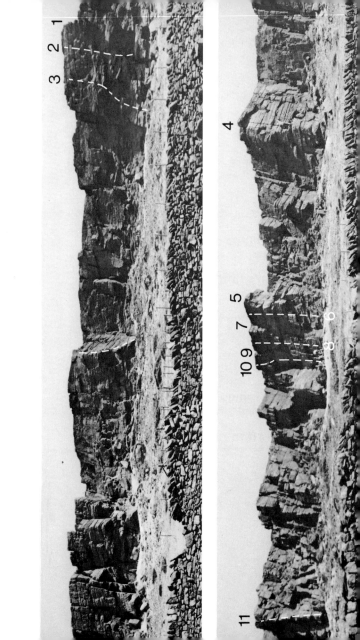

98.15 **Deep Chimney** D (2b)
A classic gritstone cleft.

98.16 The Crack 45 ft./14 m. VS (4b)
A short wall leads to a ledge. Move up and round the o/h to better holds.

98.17 Nozag 45 ft./14 m. VS (4c)
A crack leads to the R arête of the buttress. Pull on to the face and climb it awkwardly.

98.18 **Long Climb** 50 ft./15 m. D (2b)
A corner leads to the amphitheatre, with several exits.

Windgather Rocks (OS Ref 995784)
A crag which is generally easier than Castle Naze, and near the road. It has been used by generations of novices to good effect. All the climbs are about 20–30 ft./6–9 m.

South Buttress

99.1 **Crack** D (2a)
Climb it direct.

99.2 **Route 1** VS (4c)
A hard pull from the L corner of the cave leads to steep but easier ground.

99.3 **Route 2** VD (3a)
Climb the buttress front from the L, the first section being hardest.

High Buttress

*99.4 **Arête** D (2b)
Start on the R and move L to a ledge, finishing on the arête. The arête direct is 3a (VD).

99   Windgather Rocks, Kettleshulme

Middle Buttress

*99.5 **Arête**   D   (2c)
Climb to a platform and step L on to the upper wall.

*99.6 **Mississippi Crack**   VD   (3a)
The straight crack gives a good climb.

*99.7 **Chockstone Chimney**   D   (2a)
Ascend it direct.

*99.8 **Central Route**   VD   (2c)
The central crack is steep to a finish on good holds.

*99.9 **Wall Climb**   D   (2a)
The route is steepest at the final slot.

99.10 **Portfolio**   VS   (4c)
A polished wall leads to the steep wall. A boulder problem semi-mantelshelf gives an insecure finish.

North Buttress

99.11 **Arête**   D   (2b)
Climb the R side of the arête.

*99.12 **Green Crack**   S   (3b)
Go up the scoop and step R to the steep final crack.

Ramshaw Rocks   (OS Ref 019622)

The jagged, bouldery teeth of Ramshaw overlook the A53, three and a half miles north-east of Leek. Despite their numerous climbs, more varied and idiosyncratic than those of many a famous edge, they remain neglected, to the delight of their devotees. There are climbs of all standards. The rock is rough grit, green after rain but fairly quick-drying. The climbs are reached in a few minutes from the road.

100   Ramshaw Rocks South

*100.1   **The Crank**   40 ft./12 m.   VS   (4c)
Jam the awkward wide crack.

100.2   **Chockstone Chimney**   40 ft./12 m.   VD   (3b)
The chockstone is hard to reach. The climb eases above.

***100.2A   **Gumshoe**   45 ft./14 m.   E1   (5b)
Start R of 100.2 by a shallow groove in the centre of the wall. Go
up the wall to a ledge. Move up and L to finish.

100.3   **The Cannon   60 ft./18 m.   S   (3c)
TR R above the bulge and climb a juggy wall to a crack.

***100.4   **Phallic Crack**   60 ft./18 m.   VD   (3b)
The steep chimney crack is climbed from the R. The steep
sections have good holds.

100.5   **Alcatraz**   60 ft./18 m.   HVS   (5a)
Climb the thin crack with difficulty until it widens and eases.

*100.6   **The Untouchable**   45 ft./14 m.   E1   (5b)
TR L to the arête and climb the shallow crack to finish.

*100.7   **Corner Crack**   30 ft./9 m.   VD   (2c)
The crack is steep with good holds.

100.8   **Brown's Crack   50 ft./15 m.   E2   (5b)
Ascend the wall to the roof crack and pull round with difficulty.

100.9   **Prostration   50 ft./15 m.   HVS   (5a)
Climb the wall and corner to the roof. Move up with difficulty
to a steep final pull on to easier ground.

100.10   **Don's Crack   35 ft./11 m.   HVS   (5a)
Jam the fierce overhanging crack.

101.1   **Arête and Crack**   40 ft./12 m.   VD   (3c)
Pull over a lower bulge and move up to a ledge. Climb a short
crack and escape L.

101A   Ramshaw Rocks Central Area

101.2 **Bowrosin**   50 ft./15 m.   VS   (4c)
Go up the block and pull round to its R. It is easier above.

** 101.3 **Boomerang**   50 ft./15 m.   VD   (3a)
Jam the scratched crack.

101.4 **Watercourse**   60 ft./18 m.   S   (4a)
Overcome a gritty scoop. Move on to a ledge on the R and a higher ledge. TR a green scoop L to the exposed arête to finish on the nose.

*** 101.5 **Ramshaw Crack**   50 ft./15 m.   E4   (6b)
Reach the ledge from L or R. Jam the monster overhang crack – one of the Peak's hardest.

101.6 **Army Route**   50 ft./15 m.   D   (2a)
A scratched corner leads to cracks and a final short chimney.

** 101.7 **Flaky Wall**   45 ft./14 m.   VS   (4c)
The arête is climbed to a standing place on the R. Finish up a fluted wall.

*** 101.8 **The Crippler**   45 ft./14 m.   HVS   (5a)
Climb the L-slanting flake, with difficulty, to cracks above.

101.9 **Groovy Baby**   35 ft./11 m.   S   (4a)
Enter the chimney with difficulty. Above it eases.

* 101.10 **Pile Driver**   45 ft./14 m.   VS   (4c)
Start the chimney and move R to a crack. Climb it to a ledge below the top and finish steeply near the arête.

* 101.10A **The Press**   45 ft./14 m.   HVS   (5b)
Start as for 101.10. Move R at 20 ft./6 m. on to the front face. Pull in to the crack and finish up the arête. The direct start is 5c.

* 101.11 **Curfew**   40 ft./12 m.   VS   (4c)
Climb the initial o/H with difficulty to easier cracks.

*101*B   *Ramshaw Rocks North*

** *101.12* **Foord's Folly**   30 ft./9 m.   HVS   (5c)
Steep moves lead to a fierce crack. Exit R with difficulty.

Baldstones   (OS Ref 018642)
Small outcrops abound on Goldsitch Moss. All are
unfrequented and climbers should beware of antagonizing
farmers unused to their activities. This crag, the best of these
small outcrops, is best approached via a footpath from Gib Tor
(see map on page 277).

** *102.1* **Pinnacle Face**   40 ft./12 m.   VS   (4c)
Overcome the lower o/H on the R and TR L to the arête. Follow
it delicately.

** *102.2* **Pinnacle Arête**   40 ft./12 m.   HVS   (5a)
Start as 102.1, but move up R to the arête and finish up it.

** *102.3* **Goldrush**   35 ft./11 m.   E2   (5c)
Start L of the overhanging crack of 102.3, below a scoop. Go up
and move L into the scoop. At the top of the scoop, pull over a
bulge (crux) to finish.

** *102.4* **Overhanging Crack**   50 ft./15 m.   VS   (4c)
Overcome a lower bulge and climb the very steep upper
chimney.

102.5 **Ferox**   50 ft./15 m.   VD   (3c)
A lower o/H leads to a steep upper crack.

* *102.6* **Let-Out**   40 ft./12 m.   S   (4a)
A steep crack is left by moving R up rounded bulges with
difficulty.

102.7 **All Stars Wall**   20 ft./16 m.   HVS   (5b)
Climb wall L of the roof.

102.8 **Ray's Roof**   25 ft./8 m.   E6   (7a)
Start at the next buttress R, below a flaring roof. Climb to the
roof and enter the crack with difficulty. Follow the crack round
the lip with extreme difficulty.

Hen Cloud and the Roches

Ironically, the finest crags on gritstone are neither in Yorkshire
nor Derbyshire but in Staffordshire. The pyramidal mini-
mountain Hen Cloud dominates the south-west approaches to
the Peak District and gives classic climbs of every standard. An
even wider variety of climbs, bigger on average than those on
any other natural gritstone cliff in England and characterized
by a stimulating variety of rock features, is to be found on the
magnificent Upper and Lower Tiers, while the climbs of
Skyline Buttresses and the Five Clouds would be popular and
overcrowded classics in any less rock-satiated region. The rock
is pink-tinged, rough gritstone, bouldery and extremely rough
in some parts and flaky and cut by spectacular overhangs in
others. The price of the slightly 'juggy' holds is occasional
brittleness, especially on roofs.

All this is combined with spectacular scenery, ease of access
(15 minutes) and unusual fauna which inhabit the woodland.
Naturally, the cliffs are fairly popular, but they are extensive
enough to absorb considerable numbers, even on sun-trapping
summer days. Access, though legally limited, is not a practical
problem. Much of the main crag is now owned by the Peak
Park Planning Board.

Hen Cloud   (OS Ref 008616)

** 103.1 **Rainbow Crack**   60 ft./18 m.   VS   (4c)
The crack leads to a platform. Jam and layback the
overhanging crack.

** 103.2 **Great Chimney**   S   (4a)
The L crack leads to a platform. Bridge or, if short, jam the
upper chimney.

102.8   John Woodward attempting Ray's Roof, Baldstones

*** *103.3* **Bachelor's Climb**   70 ft./21 m.   VS   (4b)
A short crack leads to a ledge. The groove is awkward at first, easing before a platform. Finish as 103.2.

*** *103.4* **Bachelor's Left Hand**   70 ft./21 m.
HVS   (5a)
Move R to a crack and ascend to a hard move R and up to a slab. The fierce-looking upper crack is less difficult.

*** *103.4A* **Caricature**   70 ft./21 m.   E5   (6a)
From 20 ft./6 m. up 103.5, TR R on pockets to a crack round the arête. Follow a faint line, finishing slightly L.

** *103.5* **Rib Chimney**   60 ft./18 m.   VD   (3a)
Climb to a platform. Bridge and back and foot above.

* *103.5A* **Cool Fool**   60 ft./18 m.   E5   (6b)
Start just L, by a tiny groove which leads to a boulder. Move L and up to a ledge. Climb the arête with difficulty.

** *103.6* **Hen Cloud Eliminate**   60 ft./18 m.   HVS   (5b)
Enter a thin series of cracks and climb past a bulge to a nose-grinding final wedging chimney.

103.7 **Second's Retreat**   60 ft./18 m.   VS   (4c)
Up the groove to an overhanging funnel. Back and foot insecurely until it eases into a crack.

* *103.8* **Comedian**   60 ft./18 m.   E3   (5c)
Start a few feet R of 103.9, below a crack line. Move up and R to a break. Climb the crack and bulge, finishing up a groove. Frayed Nerve (E5, 6a) takes the wall on the R (top roped first).

103.9 **Hedgehog Crack**   40 ft./12 m.   VS   (4b)
Jam and chimney the straight crack. Fast Piping (E4, 6a) takes the wall on the L.

** *103.10* **The Arête**   100 ft./30 m.   VD   (2c)
Go up slabs to an abrupt wall. Pass this on the L (poor protection and great void) and continue more easily.

103   *Hen Cloud*

*103.11 **K2**   100 ft./30 m.   VD   (3b, 3a, 3a)
1) 40 ft./12 m. A short wall leads to a corner. Go up to a ledge.   2) 30 ft./9 m.   A crack in the wall leads to a second ledge.   3) 30 ft./9 m. Pass a bulge on the R to a chimney, which is abandoned for a final groove on the L.

*103.12 **Encouragement**   100 ft./30 m.   E1   (5b, 5b)
1) 50 ft./15 m. Go easily to a shallow groove and climb it with difficulty.   2) 50 ft./15 m. A thin crack leads to a move L and final crack.

***103.13 **Central Route**   120 ft./36 m.   (3c, 3a, 3a, 3a)
1) 25 ft./8 m. The steep crack is severe, using holds inside.   2) 40 ft./12 m. The corner leads to a terrace.   3) 25 ft./8 m. Move up on to the R end of a terrace.   4) 30 ft./9 m. A steep crack leads to the top.

V   VS   (4c)
A crack leads direct to the first stance, with rounded jamming.

103.13A **Borstal Breakout   110 ft./33 m.   E4   (4b, 5c, 6a)
1) 20 ft./60 m. Climb a crack to a grass ledge.   2) 40 ft./12 m. Go up a crack until it ends, then up to a pocket. Move R and up to a ledge.   3) 50 ft./15 m. Up the crackline above to a good ledge. Finish easily up a wall.

*103.14 **Long and Short**   110 ft./33 m.   HVS   (3b, 5b, 5b)
1) 25 ft./8 m. Climb a dirty crack to a ledge.   2) 45 ft./14 m. Climb the v-groove with difficulty to the terrace.
3) 50 ft./15 m. Take a wide crack on the L, exit R and go up a scoop, bearing L to finish.

103.15 **Roof Climb**   100 ft./30 m.   VS   (4b)
A green chimney leads to the terrace. Above, there is an easier continuation.

103.16 **Reunion Crack**   80 ft./24 m.   VS   (4c)
Swing over the first o/H and climb the easy-angled crack until it steepens. Layback to finish.

103.4A   *John Woodward on Caricature, Hen Cloud*

*** *103*.17 **Delstree**   55 ft./17 m.   HVS   (5a)
Swing over the first o/ʜ of 103.16 and ᴛʀ ʟ to an overhanging groove (delicate), or come to the same point from the ʟ and ᴛʀ ʟ likewise. Jam the crack to a balding finish.

* *103*.18 **Main Crack**   50 ft./15 m.   VS   (4c)
Jam and wedge the crack direct.

*** *103*.18A **Caesarean**   50 ft./15 m.   E4   (6b)
There is a blind flake in the wall ʟ of 103.18. Climb the flake to a break. Move ʀ and up a crack to finish. Strenuous.

** *103*.19 **En Rappel**   40 ft./12 m.   VS   (4c, 4c)
Pockets and a mantelshelf lead up to a ledge on the ʀ (belay). Tʀ ʀ to escape. It is possible to take a crack on the ʟ of the start and the wall above the ledge (4c, 4c).

103.20 **Chicken**   45 ft./14 m.   HVS   (5a)
A thin crack is left for a rib on the ʀ. Climb a short crack to a ledge. Move ʟ and climb a green scoop.
Chicken Direct   (E4, 6b) moves ʟ on to the arête and follows it.

** *103*.21 **Bulwark**   50 ft./15 m.   HVS   (5a)
Up a few feet and ᴛʀ ʟ to a scoop. Ascend and ᴛʀ ʟ to the nose (thread). The upper section is exposed and difficult and not well protected.

* *103*.21A **Slowhand**   40 ft./12 m.   E1   (5b)
A few feet ʀ of 103.21 is a crack. Climb it to its top, move up, then ʟ to finish.

The Roches – Lower Tier   (OS Ref 006623)
A bouldery, massively structured crag of ferocious jamming-cracks and pebble-dashed slabs is shrouded in mature coniferous woodland and overlooks the curious 'Rockhall' built into the boulders.

* *104*.1 **Ackit**   45 ft./14 m.   HVS   (5b)
Layback the crack and make a hard move over the bulge above the ledge.

** *104*.1A **Ascent of Man**   70 ft./21 m.   E3   (6a)
Start below a flake in the middle of the wall. Climb it, move L up a ramp and exit R.

** *104*.2 **Teck Crack**   80 ft./24 m.   HVS   (5b)
Move up the gully and TR to the base of the fierce crack (belay). Pull into the crack and climb it by layback to beyond a bulge. It is easier above.

104.3 **Lightning Crack**   60 ft./18 m.   HVS   (5a, 5a)
1) 30 ft./9 m. Enter the hanging crack and layback to the gully.   2) 30 ft./9 m. Climb the L wall of the gully with difficulty until it eases. Finish direct or escape to the R.

** *104*.3A **Hypothesis**   30 ft./9 m.   HVS   (5b)
Climb the L arête of the buttress above the path.

104.4 **Dorothy's Dilemma**   50 ft./15 m.   HVS   (5b)
From the ledge, climb the delicate arête with a thin middle section. Unprotected and serious.

** *104*.4A **Schoolies**   80 ft./24 m.   E1/2   (5a/5b)
Pull over the O/H in the buttress centre and climb direct up the middle, finishing steeply L (5a) or direct (5b).

** *104*.5 **Bengal Buttress**   75 ft./23 m.   VS   (4c)
Pull over the base of the buttress on the L and go up to a ledge on the L. TR R and climb the R edge delicately – unprotected and serious.

** *104*.6 **Crack of Gloom**   70 ft./21 m.   E1   (5b)
Jam the groove and overhanging crack to below the boulder. Back and foot L and move over the top with difficulty.

***_104.7_ **Raven Rock Gully**   95 ft./29 m.   D   (2b)
The back of the gully is climbed to a skylight – go through to a stance. An exposed finish is possible by traversing R and climbing the front of Raven Rock.

_104.8_ **Via Dolorosa   100 ft./30 m.   S   (4a)
Take the polished narrow slab to a holly ledge on the L. Leave the ledge on the L, pass a nose and go up a slab. Move L to 104.7 or move R under the chock and make an exposed layback to reach the top of the block. The finish of 104.7 is suitable.

***_104.9_ **Matinée**   70 ft./21 m.   HVS   (5a)
1) 40 ft./12 m. A steep and greasy groove is followed past a bulge. The cracks give steep jamming to the Great Flake.   2) 30 ft./9 m. Climb the obvious crack with exposed jamming to finish.

***_104.10_ **Valkyrie**   120 ft./36 m.   VS   (4b, 4c)
1) 60 ft./18 m. Climb the groove to the chimney. Move L to the Great Flake.   2) 60 ft./18 m. Hand-TR the flake and descend to its lip on the L. TR L and climb the buttress front, with initial delicate moves.

***_104.10A_ **Valkyrie Direct**   85 ft./26 m.   HVS   (5a)
Start as 104.8 to above the holly. Go up R to the O/H under the Great Flake lip. Pull over and continue as 104.10.

_104.11_ **The Swan**   70 ft./21 m.   E3   (5c)
Go up a groove to a narrow crack and ledge. Climb R to footholds and go R and reach a crack. Follow this diagonally L to finish. It is possible to TR at a higher level (5c).

_104.12_ **The Mincer   60 ft./18 m.   HVS   (5b)
A boulder problem exit R from the groove leads to ledges. TR R under the O/HS with awkward moves to enter the upper cracks. A direct start is possible.

** *104*.12A **Kicking Bird**/Smear Test   55 ft./17 m.
E3   (6a)
Start below and R of 10.12 at a bulge. Climb a short crack and
over the bulge to a small roof. Go over this and L to 104.12.
Continue to its final crack. Step R on to the slab and go up R to
finish up a shallow crack.

104.13   **Guano Gully**   40 ft./12 m.   S   (4a)
Climb a crack L of the gully line and up the groove.

* *104*.14   **Elegy**   55 ft./17 m.   E3   (5c)
Pull over the first O/H of 104.15 and fix a runner. Go L and gain
the slab. Climb it L, following the flake. Continue up the slab
with difficulty. Poorly protected.

* *104*.14A   **Clive Coolhead**   55 ft./17 m.   E4   (6b)
Starts as 104.14 to step L, then takes the bulge and slab direct.

* *104*.15   **Bulger**   45 ft./14 m.   VS   (4c)
Pull over the O/H to a ledge on the R. Enter the upper crack
awkwardly and continue more easily.

104.16   **Fledglings' Climb**   45 ft./14 m.   VD   (3a)
TR L to a crack, go up and make mantelshelves before stepping
L to a final flake.

** *104*.16A   **Carrion**   60 ft./18 m.   E2   (5c)
Go over a bulge (crux), then direct up the centre of the wall to
the top.

* *104*.17   **Kestrel Crack**   60 ft./18 m.   S   (4a)
Pull on to a slab and move L to a niche. Enter a crack above
and climb it, passing a chockstone.

** *104*.18   **Death Knell**   40 ft./12 m.   E4   (5c)
Up the blunt arête, move R and up a thin crack. Step L to
cracks and finish up them. Unprotected.

104.10   *Valkyrie Roches Lower Tier. Rod Brown and Paul Nunn*

* *104*.19 **Hunky Dory**   30 ft./9 m.   E3   (6a)
Climb a thin crack to a ledge, and finish either direct or L.

The Roches – Upper Tier   (OS Ref 005623)
The upper crag is more airy, less green and overall less fierce
than its neighbour. Here the overhangs tend to be well-
supplied with holds, and sharp holds occur on steep open faces
to give some of the best medium-standard climbing on
gritstone, as well as some unique and serious routes. The Sloth,
an exposed and remarkable overhang, is perhaps the finest of
these.

** *105*.1   **Crack and Corner**   90 ft./27 m.   S   (4a, 4a)
1) 60 ft./18 m. Make a steep jam-layback move to enter a steep
wide crack and climb it to a footpath. TR L to a steep wall and
go up to a ledge.   2) 30 ft./9 m. The crack is easy to the o/H.
Pull over with a hidden pocket and rickety flake.

** *105*.1A   **Roscoe's Wall/Round Table**   60 ft./18 m.
HVS   (5a, 5a)
1) 25 ft./8 m. 10 ft./3 m. L of 105.1 climb the middle of the wall
moving R to finish at a ledge.   2) 35 ft./11 m. From the R end
of the ledge, pull up into a L-sloping crack groove. Climb to its
top, then finish boldly R, over the o/H.

*** *105*.2   **Kelly's Shelf**   60 ft./18 m.   S   (4a)
Ascend to below the L edge of a slanting ledge. Mantelshelf on
to it and go R to a crack. Go L up the upper rounded buttress.

*** *105*.3   **Right Route**   80 ft./24 m.   VD   (3c, 3c)
1) 55 ft./17 m. Go up the slabby walls into a corner. TR L on
polished holds and brittle flakes and go up to a large ledge.
2) 25 ft./8 m. Go L to an exposed crack and ascend to the top.

** *105*.4   **Central Route**   80 ft./24 m.   S   (4a)
Climb the slab centre, moving R below the o/Hs to 105.3 to
finish. (Not well protected.)

104.19   *Hunky Dory. The Roches*

***105.5 **Pedestal Route**   90 ft./27 m.   VD   (3a)
Go up either side of the flake to a ledge (belay). Tʀ ʟ and pull
over an o/ʜ to an easier groove.

***105.6 **The Sloth**   90 ft./27 m.   HVS   (5a)
1) 45 ft./14 m. Go up to the ledge as 105.5.   2) 45 ft./14 m.
Use small holds to reach the cheeseblock. The roof start is
awkward and good holds are present thereafter for those with
the 'cool' to use them. Jam the upper crack.

105.6A **Loculous Lie   E5   (6a)
Goes ʟ from the cheeseblock to the lip, ʟ again and up the wall.
Top roped first, and 'mind-blowing'.

105.7 **Technical Slab   80 ft./24 m.   S   (4a)
Take the centre of the lower wall and the slab on widely spaced
good holds. Move ʟ to a niche and pull over the bulge to the
easier groove.

***105.8 **Black and Tans**   100 ft./30 m.   S   (3c, 3b)
1) 55 ft./17 m. Go up to a ledge and Tʀ ʀ to a sloping shelf (35
ft./11 m.), or climb the wall direct to the ledge (4b). A crack
leads to a stance on the ʟ.   2) 45 ft./14 m. The capped groove
is quitted on the ʟ. Ascend the bulgy upper wall with little
protection.

105.9 **Ruby Tuesday   100 ft./30 m.   E2   (5b, 5c)
1) 60 ft./18 m. Start as the direct on 105.8 to the ledge. Go over
the o/ʜ to the stance. Move ʟ and climb to a stance on the
ʟ.   2) 40 ft./12 m. Move ʟ and climb a steep exposed arête.

*105.10 **Jeffcoat's Buttress**   90 ft./27 m.   S   (3c, 4a)
1) 45 ft./14 m. Climb the wall and slab until forced ʟ to belay
in the chimney.   2) 45 ft./14 m. Go out ʀ to an exposed ledge
and finish via a steep crack.

105   The Roches Upper Tier, Great Slab Area

** *105.11* **Jeffcoat's Chimney**   80 ft./24 m.   D   (2a, 2a, 3a)
1) 40 ft./12 m. The chimney is climbed to a cave.
2) 20 ft./6 m. Make an awkward exit over the bulge to a ledge.
3) 20 ft./6 m. Move R on to the wall and climb it past the overlap (VD).

105.12 **Humdinger**   60 ft./18 m.   HVS   (5b)
Ascend the wall until forced L to a niche (105.13). Move R, climb the o/H, and up to a second easier bulge. Climb the wall above.

** *105.13* **Saul's Crack**   60 ft./18 m.   HVS   (5a)
Go up the crack to a niche, jam the bulging crack and reach good holds on the o/H. Pull over it and continue more easily.

* *105.13A* **Gypfast**   60 ft./18 m.   E3   (5c)
Climb L of 105.13 by the slab to a roof. Cross it at its widest point to finish up a wall.

** *105.14* **Bachelor's Buttress**   65 ft./20 m.   S   (4a)
A slab is climbed to the steep wall. Move L to a ledge near the gully and ascend the wall on the R by a series of shelves to finish up a crack or the buttress edge. Serious and unprotected.

** *106.1* **Maud's Garden**   65 ft./20 m.   VD   (3a)
The gritty slab is climbed at its centre to a wide crack above a ledge. Go up a few feet and swing on to the arête on the L to finish on good holds.

** *106.2* **Beckermet Slab**   65 ft./20 m.   D   (2b)
Move L on to the arête and up to a break. The upper slab is very worn. Poorly protected.

** *106.2A* **West's Wallaby**   75 ft./23 m.   VS   (4b)
Climb a crack to a large jammed block. TR R on jams and round the arête. Finish up slabs.

* *106.3* **Walleroo**   65 ft./20 m.   E2   (5c)
A crack leads to the hanging block. Move up L over the bulge and into a groove. Continue direct.

106   The Roches Upper Tier, Maud's Garden-Chicken Run

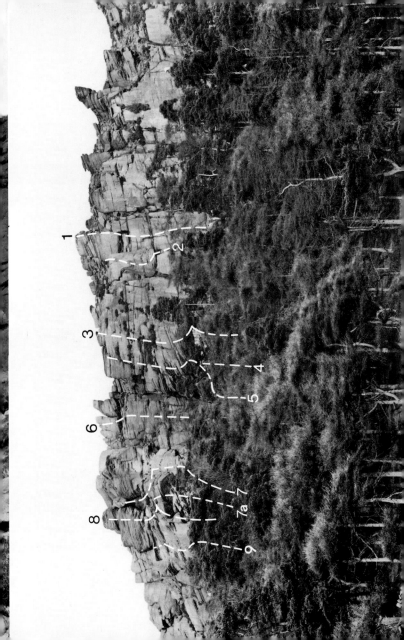

106.4 ** **Wombat**   65 ft./20 m.   E1   (5b)
A short groove leads to the roof. Move R to a thread and cross the roof on doubtful flakes. A short crack leads to easier ground.

106.5 **Capitol**   65 ft./20 m.   S   (4a)
Climb a crack and TR R under the o/h to a short crack. Continue more easily.

106.6 **Heather Slab**   45 ft./14 m.   VD   (2c)
The slab is climbed in the centre, finishing just L of a short crack.

106.7 *** **Inverted Staircase**   45 ft./21 m.   D   (2a)
1) 50 ft./15 m. Go up R following slabs to a groove and climb it to ledges on the L.   2) 20 ft./6 m. Squirm through a chimney.

106.7A * **Simpkins' Overhang**   45 ft./14 m.   E4   (5c)
Climb the large roof L of 106.7. Cross it on a flake that leads R to a final long hard pull to finish.

106.8 * **Demon Wall**   55 ft./17 m.   S   (3c, 4a)
1) 35 ft./11 m. Pull over the o/h and climb a corner to the ledge on the R (sandy).   2) 20 ft./6 m. Make difficult polished moves up the face.

106.9 *** **Fern Crack**   60 ft./18 m.   D   (3a, 2c)
1) 35 ft./11 m. The bulging wall is climbed on good holds. Move L and up to a shelf. Thread belay.   2) 25 ft./8 m. Go L to a recess and climb a crack on its L or a wall to the R.

106.10 **Chicken Run**   35 ft./11 m.   D   (2a)
The lower slab leads to a ledge. Make a high step to start the upper section and continue up a steeper wall and crack – polished.

The Five Clouds – The Third Cloud

The central buttress of the Five clouds stands behind a farm building and should be approached from a point a little way along the road, avoiding vulnerable walls.

* *107*.1 **Flower Power Arête**   50 ft./15 m.   E2   (5c)
Up the rib L of the cave to a ledge. Make a long reach to a layback crack and climb it to a ledge. Finish up a corner crack.

** *107*.2 **Crabbie's Crack**   55 ft./17 m.   VS   (5a)
A green groove leads to the crack and a ledge on the L. Go L and climb a cracked wall. Other variations are possible.

*** *107*.3 **Appaloosa Sunset**   55 ft./17 m.   E2   (5c)
Start up a shallow corner. Follow holds up and R to a long reach for a good hold. Finish direct. The direct start is E2 (6b).

*** *107*.4 **Rubberneck**   55 ft./17 m.   HVS   (5a)
Bridge the scoop to a crack and climb to a bulge. Continue, going R to a ledge and finish up a short wall.

Harsten Rock – Churnet valley   (OS Ref SK 032477)

Though this cliff is not in the Peak District, it is nevertheless one of the hidden gems of the region's climbing and one of the more spectacular buttresses on grit. A pinnacle, it is composed of sandy red gritstone, with steep walls plunging into lower bulges. It is approached from the A52 Stoke–Ashbourne road about 500 yds./460 m. north-east of the junction with the B5033. A track leads to a farm, beyond which there are several buttresses before the Harsten Rock itself, which is last of the series.

** *108*.1 **Via Trita**   45 ft./14 m.   HVS   (5a)
A thin crack and wall leads to the O/H. Step L, mantelshelf and finish up rippled holds.

*** *108.2* **The Helix**   80 ft./24 m.   HVS   (5a)

Climb the crack for 6 ft./2 m. and TR L beneath the bulge. Step up and L (crux) and continue up ripples to a sloping ledge on the arête. Go L along the ledge to a steep groove and climb it to the top.

** *108.3* **DNA**   60 ft./18 m.   E2   (6a)

Climb the scoop to a prow. Move L along a break, then up to the next break. Finish up an easy crack.

108.4 **Impending Doom**   60 ft./18 m.   HVS   (5b)

Move into a niche and ledge on the L. A flake is abandoned with difficulty by a move R to a crack. Climb this and move L. Make a difficult move to a ledge and finish up a recess.

The Old Man of Mow   (OS Ref   SJ 858576)

This unique quarried pinnacle resides in a hollow below the folly landmark at Mow Cop, south of Congleton.

*** *109.1* **Spiral Route**   65 ft./20 m.   S   (4a)

From the ledge, move up L and round the corner to an easy angled slab. Move L round the corner and up the slab to the notch (PB). Move R round the corner and up a final slab.

** *109.2* **Direct Route**   55 ft./17 m.   HVS   (5a)

Climb the groove through the O/H to the slab. Move L on to a steep face and climb it (dubious holds) until the L edge can be used to reach holds above. Finish as for 109.1.

** *109.3* **Alsager Route**   55 ft./17 m.   HVS   (5a)

A slab is climbed (bad rock) to a groove leading to the notch (PB). The groove is taken direct.

** *109.4* **Cambridge Crack**   35 ft./11 m.   VS   (4c)

Climb the overhanging crack to the ledge. The top can be reached by following 109.2. The abseil descent is awkward and requires care to ensure that the rope runs freely.

Select Bibliography

Rock Climbs on the Peak. BMC Peak Guides Sub-
Committee Official Series

Volume 1 The Sheffield–Stanage Area, ed. Eric
Byne (1963, reprint 1970)

Volume 2 The Saddleworth–Chew Area, ed.
Eric Byne (1965)

Volume 3 The Sheffield–Froggatt Area, ed.
Eric Byne (1965)

Volume 4 The Chatsworth–Gritstone Area,
compiler Eric Byne, ed. A. Moulam, J Neill,
P Nunn (1970)

Volume 5 The Northern Limestone Area,
compiler and ed. Paul Nunn (1969)

Volume 6 The Bleaklow Area, compiler Eric
Byne, ed. Paul Nunn (1971)

Volume 7 The Kinder Area, compiler Eric
Byne, ed. Paul Nunn (1972)

Volume 8 The Southern Limestone Area,
compiler and ed. Paul Nunn (1970)

Volume 9 The Roches and Churnet Area,
compilers D Salt and C Foord (1974)

Volume 1 Stanage Area, B Griffiths and Alan
Wright (1976)

Volume 2 Chew Valley, B Whittaker (1976)

Volume 3 Froggatt Area, D Gregory (1978)

Volume 4 Northern Limestone, Chris Jackson
(1980)

Volume 5 Derwent Valley, Jim Ballard and
Ernie Marshall (1981)

Volume 6 Staffordshire Area, Mike Browell,
Steve and Brian Dale, and Nick Longland
(1981)

Peak District: New Routes. Gary Gibson
(1981)

Peak Supplement. Gary Gibson (1983)

Stanage (BMC 4th series). G. Milburn (1983)

Derwent Gritstone (BMC 4th series). G
Milburn (1983)

Mountain Rescue. The Mountain Rescue
   Committee.
Safety on Mountains. CCPR.

*For up-to-date information, consult the following
   magazines:* Mountain. 1969–0000 (bi-
   monthly)
Climber (monthly)
High. 1982 (monthly)

Map   For most of the area: The Peak District
   Tourist Map (HMSO).